PRIVATE MONEY SECRETS

THE UNDERGROUND PLAYBOOK TO RAISING LOTS OF MONEY FOR YOUR REAL ESTATE DEALS

KEITH YACKEY

Visit the Official Website at: www.KeithYackey.com

Printed in the United States of America

First Printing: October 2020

Keith Yackey

ISBN: 978-0-578-76972-1

Keith Yackey books may be purchased for educational, business or sales promotional use. Special discounts are available on quantity purchases. For more information, please call or write.

Telephone (800) 269-6818; Email: support@keithyackey.com

For orders by U.S. trade bookstores and wholesalers, please contact Keith Yackey's assistant at the phone or email address listed above.

DISCLAIMER

The Publisher has strived to be as accurate and complete as possible in the creation of this book. This book is not intended for use as a source of professional, financial or investing advice. All readers are advised to seek services of competent professionals in the real estate investment field.

Readers are cautioned to rely on their own judgment about their individual circumstances to act accordingly.

While all attempts have been made to verify information provided in this publication, the Publisher assumes no responsibility for errors, omissions, or contrary interpretation of the subject matter herein. Any perceived slights of specific persons, peoples, or organizations are unintentional. This book details the author's own personal experiences and opinions. The author is not licensed as a psychologist, or psychiatrist.

The author and publisher are providing this book and its contents on an "as is" basis and make no representations or warranties of any kind with respect to this book or its contents. The author and publisher disclaim all such representations and warranties, including for example warranties of merchantability and educational or medical advice for a particular purpose. In addition, the author and publisher do not represent or warrant that the information accessible via this book is accurate, complete or current.

Except as specifically stated in this book, neither the author or publisher, nor any authors, contributors, or other representatives will be liable for damages arising out of or in connection with the use of this book. This is a comprehensive limitation of liability that applies to all damages of any kind, including (without limitation) compensatory; direct, indirect or direct, indirect or consequential damages; loss of data, income or profit; loss of or damage to property and claims of third parties.

You understand that this book is not intended as a substitute for consultation with a licensed legal or financial professional. Before you begin any new venture, you must consult a licensed professional to ensure that you are doing what's best for your situation.

This book provides content related to educational, financial and real estate investing topics. As such, use of this book implies your acceptance of this disclaimer.

Dedicated to My Mom.
Without you turning to me that one day
and saying "you could do that", I may never have.
Because of you, I am living a life of no regrets.

Ready to Explode Your
Real Estate Investing Business?

Get IMMEDIATE Access to a

FREE

"Private Money Secrets"
On-Demand Class Today!

www.PrivateMoneySecretsBook.com/class

TABLE OF CONTENTS

ACKNOWLEDGEMENTS

Writing a book is something a lot people say they want to do, but never do. Now I can say, I did. But I didn't do it alone. I have amazing people around me. In fact I say "We" a lot, knowing it is never just me. Because I grew up playing team sports this has been ingrained in me.

First, to my Creator. You have given me breath. As long as I have it within in me I will honor your guidance the best way I know how. Please never stop speaking to me, for your words are my life. Our Gummy tent meetings have been the most precious moments for me on this earth. I look forward to them every week and approach them with great anticipation, reverence and deep awe.

I want to thank my life partner Jesse Marquez. The best human I know for me. You are a god send and life without you would be boring and unfulfilling. Thanks for being my best friend and lover. Your unwavering love for me and our daughter is nothing short of inspiring.

Next is my long time friend and true partner in crime, Aaron Hovivian. Going on 27 years knowing each other and you truly have been my "Jonathan". Words cannot express my depth of gratitude for all you have been to me. All my business dealings have your fingerprint on it and for that I'm eternally grateful.

The next group of men have been my "four horsemen" as it were, even though there are more than four, in business and life. I plan on walking side by side with you well into our 90s. My truest friends.

Pete Vargas you were my first real "friend" in the experts space and you have been the biggest megaphone and cheerleader for me ever since. Our bond is unshakable and you truly have been a Rock for me. You truly are PV3! Your drive to serve and win at the same time is awe inspiring. White and Brown till we die!

Dan Martell you have shown me kindness and ambition can coexist harmoniously. The laughter we have shared is still medicine for my soul. You exemplify the word entrepreneur and our first time meeting in the hot tub is the stuff of legends. Our frequent FaceTime sessions leave a smile on my face for the entire day. I love you man!

Garrett J White you have etched an indelible positive mark on my soul and my life. We surf almost every day and what I have learned from you has left me a changed man. You have made me laugh harder than anyone I know and also have stoked a fire in me like never before. Whatever I go after in life I can hear you yelling in my head "Yeah You!" MARAPY brothers for life, Hold my beer.

Taylor Welch you are a gift man. I have learned more about leadership through our friendship than all the leadership books combined. This is just the start and our Creator has so much in store for us. Honored to call you a true friend and I love dissecting downloads with you. I hope Nashville gets a wave pool someday soon.

Wade T Lightheart, AKA "Thunderfelt" you are my brother from another mother. 16 years strong! Screaming Zebras forever! My health now and in the future thanks you. I hope you and I play pool in heaven and you color commentate the whole thing, forever!

Garrett Gunderson you inspire me man. You encouraged me to do this a while ago and I thank you for that. Our talks have a special place in my heart and our journey of making people laugh is something I will cherish forever. Love you man.

Everyone on the team I love you. Terryn you make everything run smoothly. Bryan you make sure everyone is happy and taken care of. Darren and Jonathan you show people the way. Jesh, Savannah and Lynsee you are an amazing support. Leon, Yasmin and Kristin you make sure people see me and my message. Bryce you make sure my crazy rants end up in a polished fashion for the podcast. For that I thank each of you!

Dave Woodward thank you for writing the Foreword and for being such a true friend. You have known me from way back and we are still great friends. That says a lot and my heart swells with deep gratitude that you are a part of this project with me in this way.

Travis Cody thank you for bringing this book to life. It was a long road because of my delays but you patiently guided me through the process. I'll forever thank you.

To every teacher I have learned from , thank you. I have now in turn taught others. To all my entrepreneur friends, I have learned as much from you, or more, as you have from me. And to those who have thrown rocks at me, I have built something awesome with them, thank you for the motivation and the materials.

Lastly, I want to thank every mentor I have ever had. Some were great leaders and some were great examples of bad leadership. I have learned so much from both. And for that I thank you.

FOREWORD

*by **Dave Woodward**,*
CEO of Clickfunnels

"Why would I ever give you money?"

Those are the 7 words that shattered my dreams of becoming a real estate investor.

Have you ever watched HGTV house flipping shows and thought… "I know I can do that. It can't be that hard." That was me in 2009. I was trying to dig out of the financial crisis of 2007 and 2008. I saw tons of opportunities all around me as people were walking away from their homes. I saw so many trashed houses and knew this was the answer to my prayers.

I had no experience except for watching hours of HGTV house flipping shows. But I knew I had to find a way to make it work.

I figured if the people I saw on TV could do it then I could too. The only problem was I knew it would take money… money I did not have. Everyone talks about using "OPM," other people's money, but where do you find the people with money? More importantly, what do you say to convince them to believe in you and the deals you want to do.

Necessity was my driving force. I had to find a way to make it work. Fortunately over time I did figure it out and was able to flip hundreds of homes over the next couple of years. Unfortunately, the school of hard knocks takes way too much time and is a brutal teacher. I only wish there had been someone with years of experience raising private money who could simplify the process. Someone who could make it easy enough for anyone willing to do the work to be able to raise the hundreds of thousands of dollars that it takes to be successful in this business.

Fortunately for you, there is. The book you hold in your hands is the answer you've been looking for.

I've personally watched Keith Yackey raise millions of dollars to fund his own deals. (You'd expect he can do it, to write a book about it.) But Keith's ability to raise money won't fund your deals directly. What really matters to you is not that Keith can raise money. What matters is that he has taught thousands to be able to do it, and now you.

Keith's skill in simplifying the process while help-ing increase your confidence to raise money is second to none. He has the ability to make the nerve wracking, fear laden experience of raising money not only simple but *actually* achievable. His Private Money Process and 4Cs will help you raise money no matter what level of experience you have. I've known Keith for over 10 years and he is the real deal. He lives what he preaches and cares about those who turn to him for his knowledge and wisdom.

Are you brand new to investing? Never done a real estate deal in your life? No problem! Keith makes it as simple as painting by numbers. When you are done you will feel that you've created a masterpiece. If you have a lot of experience, Keith's content will take your money raising skills to a new level. You may find yourself having access to too much money.

There is an art and a science to raising private money. Keith explains both in this book.

If you take action and implement his easy "action steps" at the end of each chapter you will be able to raise all of the money you need to fund all of the deals you could ever imagine or dream of doing.

I only wish I had found someone like Keith when I was learning to raise money. He would have saved me tons of time and money. The great part about learning to raise money is if you can do it, you can do anything. Excuses about money appear to be one of the major reasons most people never reach their dreams. Don't let this be you. Take massive action and implement what you find in the following pages. You will be amazed at the doors of opportunity that swing wide open for you.

INTRODUCTION

My name is Keith Yackey. I'm the founder of Private Money Pro and the creator of The Private Money Process, a step-by-step system designed to teach you how to raise all the cash you will ever need for your real estate deals. Congratulations on picking up this book. When you learn this step-by-step system, you will:

- Create credibility Even if you have never done a deal before
- Understand how to put together your content in a way that an investor wants to see it
- Walk with confidence when talking with private money lenders
- Learn how to close the deal with style
- Connect to the right people who have private money that want to invest

The result? Your ability to raise private money will go through the roof. You'll go from noob to a pro, ultimately becoming an expert. In the last seven years, I have raised over 50 million dollars and enjoyed speaking on stage with some of the biggest names in the world. I've taught Major League Baseball pitchers, NFL defensive backs, highly decorated war heroes, extreme sports stars and actors. My step-by-step system will change the way you see the process of raising private money. Even if you've already started down this road, I will help you get to the next level—where you can raise all the money you could ever want.

I'm excited for you to take this step, and I'm excited to be your mentor. I know that this process is going to serve you well. I look forward to hearing all of the great stories of the successes you'll have after going through this book. Before we get started, however, I have to provide a little disclaimer. I am not an attorney. I am not offering you legal advice, and I will say many times in this book that you need to talk with your attorney. The steps you'll read about are simply my ideas and my experiences. I know they will serve you well because this process is what's helped me become very successful. But again, nothing I have to offer here should be considered legal advice.

Now that we have that out of the way, I want to salute you for following in the footsteps of many great people. When successful people want to learn something, they hire the best to teach them. What you've done right now by purchasing this book is to announce, "I hire the best. I learn from the absolute best expert." I will show the documents you need to use. I will show you the mindset you have to have and the demeanor. I will show you how to communicate and how to talk with lenders to get the results you seek.

I've seen students of mine start off downright clumsy, yet when I showed them these principles with just a couple of tweaks, *boom!* They went off to be a great success, flipping a hundred homes. One guy I met, for example, was doing one home at a time. I ended up showing him my system—how I do multiple deals and how to leverage hard money, private money, gap money, and how it all works. That guy went on to do over a *thousand real estate deals.* I'm so proud of him.

What Is Private Money?

Private money is any funds people invest with you— whether it be as a partner or as a lender—to do a real estate deal. It can be friends and family. It can be spouses. It can be cousins. It can be the doctor, lawyers, earthmovers, timber people, you name it. However, there are certain types of people that I want to teach you how to contact so you can get the best results in the shortest amount of time. You'll soon learn the best spots to go for raising private money, where people will be more receptive. I'll explain where to go, what to say, how you should act, and how you should position yourself. All of these things are very key when you're raising private money.

There are four important factors—that I call the 4 C's—involved in raising private money:

1. **Credibility.** Are you credible? Are you a scammer or are you a fraud? There's a lot of information out there. Some of it isn't true, of course, but you have to take care of your reputation on the internet nevertheless. We will explore how to create credibility and how to have people perceive you as an expert. So People will perceive you however you *want* them to perceive you. I'm going to show you how to create good credibility. You can do it with deals, of course, but I'm going to show you how to do it even without deals via proof of concept. Credibility is massively important, so we will get deep into how to create your credibility: what it takes and what things you can do to up your credibility.

2. **Good Content.** Good content shows investors why a deal will work. To help investors see that a deal is a no-brainer, we will explore what good content should look like. I'll explain the items an investor package should include so your deal looks solid. You'll learn how to create a past deal packet to build

your credibility. If you do not yet have a history of completed deals, we'll talk about how to include what other people have done and how you can create credibility off of that information.

When I show you how to build an investor packet, you're going to see me go into what I call "FBI mode." I get down to the nitty-gritty details so my information is content-rich and true. Investors look at it and say, "I'm interested in this."

3. **Confidence.** If you know you're a credible source for deals, you'll project the right attitude and confidence. You're not some evil, malicious, or fraudulent person. No, you have credibility and the right documents, whether they be deeds of trust, a mortgage, or promissory notes. You understand a joint venture agreement, a JVA: what they are, how they work, and how they are structured. When you understand how all this works, your confidence level will be high because you know you're offering a good deal. You know that it's a deal that should be funded and will be funded.

If you seem needy or desperate, nobody will want to lend with you. Your mindset has to say, "I've got an opportunity for you." We will explore how to portray yourself as the one person that they want to invest in. You can literally go from somebody who says, "I can't raise money" to the person who says, "I have more money than I need. I need to go find more deals."

The reason why half the people don't succeed is because they're around negative people and what does that negativity do? It buries your confidence. Who are you letting influence your life? You need to be in a good state of mind and we're going to go through how to create unshakable confidence.

4. **Closing Ability.** You have to be able to close. You can talk to everybody in the world and they can all say, "Yes, I want to do a deal with you," but unless you can get them to commit the funds and then actually send the funds, you'll never get anything done. There's a specific closing sequence I will teach you. A lot of people get confused about what to do next. Because they have the fear of the unknown, they stop. It's that inaction that causes the paralysis by analysis.

In this book, we will drill down on each of the four. Credibility: What's it like? Content: How you create it, gather it, and crystallize it so investors want to partner with you? Confidence: How do you create it? What kind of mental gymnastics do you need to go through? Who are your influencers? Closing: How do you actually get them to bring you the money?

This is The Private Money Process. Having been one of the guys who has created some advanced programs for a lot of gurus out there while staying in the shadows, it's fun to step into the light and say, "Here's the process." Here's how you can take raising private money to a whole new level that will cause your business to grow by leaps and bounds.

For all the resources I mention in this book go to www.privatemoneysecretsbook.com I have everything you need there.

I also have cool videos there, document samples and other helpful things you will want to have when raising dump truck loads of private money.

CHAPTER 1

CONNECTION

I had finally done it. I had finally mailed out some mailers to see if I could find private investors. After looking up the information in the public recorder's office, I put together a letter that I thought might entice somebody to want to call me and do a deal.

Then, it happened. I received a phone call thanks to my letter.

A man said, "Hey, I got your letter. I'm a private lender who does deals around here and would love to see what you're up to."

I said, "Great! It's Tuesday and they've got a great Taco Tuesday deal going on downtown. Do you want to meet me there?"

When I met with him, I tried to keep it personal: friendly, fun, and lighthearted. The goal was to connect, to build some rapport. I asked him basic questions and then asked more probing ones to really get a feel for who he was and what made him tick.

Eventually, he asked, "What are you up to? What kind of deals are you working on?"

I told him and asked, "What type of returns do you typically get?" He let me know.

So, I learned we were in the same ballpark. We just had to do deals together.

When you're making a new connection from your mailers, get referred to by other investors, or friends or family members say they want to work with you, keep it casual at first. Think of it like dating. You're not going to pick somebody up who's brand new from the bar and go home with them that night. Instead, you have a first date to learn more about each other.

It's the same concept here. Talk about your expectations, their desires and what they're wanting to accomplish. Learn where they want to go and what they want to do. You're seeing if there is an alignment between you. It's a chance for you to see if you want to work with them by getting a sense of the way they're treating the wait staff. You are finding out if they're a pain in the ass.

Remember, you have options. You're interviewing *them* to see if they're a good fit. When you have that attitude, you'll do well. Tell yourself, "I know this isn't the last investor on planet Earth. If this guy or gal says

no, there are plenty more who want to invest with me."
You will come off with a calm air about you, and people like that. Again, maintain the stance of, "I don't need you, but I'd like to work with you and it looks like this might be a good fit."

Keep it casual. Stay human. Be personal and personable. It will help you in the end.

When you get the four C's down—your credibility, content, confidence, and closing ability— the next question is where to connect with private money investors. Where do they congregate? Where can you go to meet them? There's no magic bullet; there is no one way. If your business has only one source of leads and that source dries up, where's your business? I'm going to give you a list and explain to you where and how I connect.

My favorite spots to encounter private money investors, hard money or both include:
- Title and Escrow Agents referrals
- Realtors and Brokers
- Seminars and conferences
- Real estate associations and clubs
- Real estate Meetup groups
- Craigslist
- Private Money Pro list
- Courthouse steps
- REO auctions

- Public records
- Financial Planners
- Other Business owners

Escrow and Title Companies

It dawned on me when I was lending money in the Carolinas that I didn't need any of my own paperwork. I just told the para legal (gal who worked for the closing attorney) here is the amount, the interest rate and when it is due. She drafted everything from the promissory note to the mortgage. I just signed it and wired the money. Then it hit me, She is the hub that all spokes connect to in every single real estate deal. She sees more private money paperwork than anyone. She knows who is lending what and at what percentage.

Everything flows through the Escrow Agent (Closing Attorney in some states). They know everyone and are often not recognized for their efforts in getting deals closed. What an opportunity for you to be different and stand out.

I have taught this one simple technique to my clients and it is responsible for many millions raised. Simply reach out to them and say " Hey I know you see more private money documents than anyone. I am looking to expand my business with private money. I was wondering if you could introduce me to some of the private money lenders you have worked with. If we end up doing anything together I will make it worth your wild."

Usually you will get one of a few answers. They will say "Yes I am happy to make that intro" or maybe they will say "Here is there number, tell them I gave it to you" Or they will say "I'll pass your number along and if they are interested they can reach out to you.

The intro is the strongest, but all of them will move you forward to talking to more real private lenders. The escrow agent or closing attorney will be your best friend and is a great place to start your journey. You don't even have to have a prior relationship with them. It just helps if you do.

Seminars and Conferences

In the past when people have bought my training packages, I gave them two free tickets to my live event because I know it will be one of the most powerful seminars they'll ever experience. Lenders are there to connect—friends of mine who lend on properties. Seminar and conferences for learning about real estate investing can be quite large and people pay a good sum of money to go to them. They can be a fabulous place to meet those with money who want to do deals. At a seminar, you are surrounded by like-minded people who are all excited about the same thing you are. You all have the same goal, dream, and aspiration to make money in real estate. Some of these seminars can be expensive. But that's okay because you want to build my business for the long term. There is no quick fix. I will go to the ends of the earth to make sure that things are done right in my deal. Even if it costs me money, I want to make sure I have a good relationship and a reputation amongst those who do business with me.

Seminars are incubators of joint venture agreements and of lender-borrower relationships. It's a huge team going in the same direction. Everybody's on the bus together, but sometimes you'll think, "Well, I go to these seminars to learn but I don't have any money. I'm not really an asset." That's not true. Maybe you have lots of time. A guy with lots of time but not a whole lot of money is the perfect match for the person who has very little time but lots of money. This is a recipe for success. It's called joint venturing. This is how 95 percent of all people get started.

Real estate conferences, seminars, and training events will be the most powerful place you'll ever connect or congregate with people with money. Their mindset is already going in the direction you're headed, and that is important because this is a relationship business. If you go solicit anybody to give you money for one of your investments, you could be violating the law. The SEC says you can't go solicit investors. You can't take out a billboard that says, "I want to give you a 12 percent return on your money. Invest with me." There has to be what's called a prior relationship involved. Training events such as real estate investing seminars create a lot of prior relationships.

Clubs and Associations

A club or association is a group that might meet on a monthly basis. There are a lot of real estate clubs, some are called associations. A club or association may cost you $100 to $200 a year. Sometimes, it's just a per-meeting fee of around $15. I actually like to pay for these memberships, and I'll tell you why. Any time you have a barrier to entry to get anything, you're going to meet a higher quality person on the other side of the barrier.

It always blows my mind to think most people will gladly pay $15 or more to go to the movies and sit there and veg out. Believe me, I love movies as much the next person, but it strikes me as odd to then hear people say, "I don't want to pay $15 to go to a real estate investing club which could possibly introduce me to somebody who says they want to fund my deals." It doesn't make sense to me. Where our priorities? Pay the $15 to go to the real estate gathering. Clubs and associations are generally less expensive than seminars or conferences.

Use Meetup groups. All you have to do is type in, "Meetup group private money," "Meetup group hard money," or "Meetup group real estate" and you'll see there are some groups out there that are thoroughly engaged. They'll have 300 to 500 members. There are lenders in these groups as well as private money people, hard money people, investors, and wholesalers. If you go to this Meetup and have the four Cs mastered—your credibility, your content, your confidence, and your ability to close—you will raise tons and tons of money.

Also in the more digital age you can look up the organizer and just reach out to them individually and ask them if they can connect you to anyone that they know lending private money in their group. I look at them like pastors of their congregation. They know who is doing what in their group. They are a huge resource for you.

Craigslist

I like Craigslist. There are two ways you can use it. The first is to simply look for ads. There are ads in there saying "I'm a private money lender," or "I'm a hard money lender." Try different search words. I found one of my biggest private investors ever on a Craigslist. That's why I feel so passionate about it because it is an amazing place to connect.

Another thing you can do is place ads. You've got to be careful how you do this because you want to build a relationship first. Your ad can say something to the effect of, "I have amazing wholesale deals. Looking for cash buyers." Then say, "Call me or respond to my email." The reason this ad works so well is that the only people who will call you are people that have cash or use hard money. They have connections. You're going to get a hold of people who actually have cash and build your list of buyers.

A wholesale deal, for example, is when you put a property on a contract and you sell that contract off. For a fee, you give someone else the right to buy the property that you want to sell. Place an ad saying you're looking for cash buyers. When someone calls, say, "I've got one deal where I'm not wholesaling it off. I'm looking for cash, a private investor. Let me know if you're interested." We're always wanting to give somebody an opportunity to invest their money. Say, "Let me give you an opportunity. We can joint venture together; we can partner together to make some money."

If you place an ad that says, "I have amazing wholesale deals looking for cash buyers," this is an ad that will garner some great results. You never know who's going to call you. I like Craigslist is because it shows which people are active. Responses can be immediate. It costs

$25, sometimes, to post. Those who pay are actively pursuing Craigslist are ready to do a deal.

Courthouse Steps

On the courthouse steps, who is there buying real estate? People with cash or people who are buying for people with cash. So, if your goal is to try and be around as many people as you possibly can who have money and like real estate, that's where they'll be.

When you go to the courthouse steps, there is a pack mentality. You're going to be the new kid on the block. When you go, you'll see people there with their little foldout lawn chairs and a little covering so they can be in the shade. They're going to have their tablets and all these different things that they do. Everybody knows one another. They're like, "Oh yeah, there's the guy with the visor. He's here every other day."

They know when a new person comes in. You have to learn how to be able to assimilate yourself into a new situation. Just show up so they start to become familiar with you. Be the person who thinks about building your business long term. I took a couple of students there one time and I was able to raise a few hundred thousand dollars with one conversation. But that's because I've been trained on how to build rapport and how to communicate. My credibility was high, my confidence was high,

I knew my content, and I could rattle off numbers with no problem.

The courthouse steps are a great place to meet people who have cash and are buying deals. What if they will only want to buy their own deal? Don't worry about that. You know how many private investors I have met who have so much money that they buy their own deals *and* lend to others to go do deals? A lot. When you go back and look at deals that you've seen, the private investor often makes as much, or sometimes even more than you do when you flip your deal. And he did zero work; he just put his cash up. Yes, he's putting his cash at risk, but he's not doing any of the work. There's that give and take. Don't think that because you go to the courthouse steps, you'll only meet people who want to buy their own deals. They will lend or they will know who lends. If you're new in the game, you can meet people and say, "Hey, I've got this deal." What are they looking for? They're looking for deals!

You have two options. You can bring them a deal you want a wholesale off to them. That's how you can make some quick cash. Or, you can go down there and say, "Hey, I've got a deal. Would you like to fund it?" Maybe you know you think you should be 50-50 but they want more of the prize because they're lending you and you're new to the game. That's fine. I look at this as the cost of doing business. It's the pay to play type mentality. Don't be afraid of that. Eventually, as you become more known, you will get access to cheaper and cheaper money.

REO Auctions

The courthouse steps are for a property that's going into foreclosure. The bank will auction it off to anyone. This gives the person who defaulted the chance to remedy their loan. If the property doesn't sell at the courthouse steps, then goes into what's called an REO auction. You can find a lot of home auctions in the United States at auction.com or Hubzu.

But they don't just do it online because they know that if you can fuel that competitive fire to outbid another person, the price drives up drastically. This happened with one of the first fourplexes I ever bought. There was a lady next to me, maybe two or three seats down, and she kept bidding against me. I ended up paying more than I wanted for the property. It was a good deal but I ended up paying more for the property than that I wanted to, all because we get competitive.

More importantly, who is at that REO auction? You have people there that maybe only have $100k or $200k. But if you go in there as the expert who understands how to do real estate and say, "What are you up to?" you can start a useful conversation. Someone might reply, "We're trying to buy property," giving you the opportunity to say, "I've done x number of deals in the area. Maybe we should joint venture on some stuff?" Maybe they don't know how to buy or what to buy. Maybe they're simply there and unclear exactly how the whole game works. If you've been trained and know exactly how to do it, they will want to partner with you.

If you build that rapport and have the credibility, the content, and confidence on cue, you'll find you'll be able to close people at an REO auction.

Public Records

You can find private money investors by researching public real estate and loan records. This information is available to any who wants to use it if they know how to find it. It is such a great way to find a new connection, but it's a little bit more work than everything I explained earlier in this chapter. However, this work is worth it if you're building your business for longevity.

Here's how it works: Let's say person A is the lender, the mortgagee. Then you have the borrower, person B, the mortgagor. What happens in public records is if lender A does a mortgage with borrower B, it's recorded. The recorder's office is—just as the name implies—where they keep all the public records.

There's a bunch of websites out there with this information. The best website that I know of is called Publicrecordsources.com. Pick your state, you pick your county. Look for the button or tab that says deeds, recordings, liens, mortgages, or deeds of trust. If you click on that, it will take you to the website of the county. You can look up stuff by parcel number. Click on the document tab. It takes you to another website. You put in MTG for a mortgage or deed of trust.

Two dates appear and you can do a search within a given span of time. Let's say the last 30 days. Once you input the dates, you'll get brought into a screen with line upon line upon line of mortgages that were recorded in the last 30 days.

Go through the list. You'll see both the borrower's name and who did the mortgage. Don't click if you see that Wells Fargo did a loan. Wells Fargo isn't a private investor. But you will see in there a name like Jan Peters. If there is a hyperlink, click on it. It often has the actual mortgage right there. It's the actual document. Guess whose information on the document? You have the mortgagee: their address, sometimes they even have their phone number. You have to weed through long lists of information to find private investors, but you can learn a ton. You'll see people lending 3 percent money for 360 months. That's crazy. That's super cheap. That's the kind of person you want to meet. Is there a lot of work involved in this? Absolutely. But how qualified of a lead do you want to get?

You can then send letters. You put a mailing campaign together and develop a relationship with these individuals. You talk to them about what you do and say, "Hey, let's get together. Let's talk shop." This is a long way around the barn. But you can do this all from the comfort of your home in your PJs with a cup of coffee next to you. If you can't find this level of detail for your county online, all you have to do is go to the county courthouse records department. It might even be called the recorder's office. Say, "I want to look up mortgages" or deeds of trust.

Each state is different regarding which instrument they use to secure the real property. Some are mortgage states, some are deeds of trust. They're pretty much the exact same document. They'll actually pull up a list and they'll print it out for you and charge you for it. I've heard of people spend three or four hours and walk out with 30 or 40 private lenders that they can contact. Doing a public record search can be so fruitful and profitable for you.

Warm Leads

Lastly, there are your family and your friends. These are usually the people that my students are most afraid to talk to. They've seen you grow up or they know this is a new business venture for you. Maybe you've had a few business ventures before that didn't pan out so well, so you're super nervous about talking with them. I'm going to show you how you can get rid of all of that anxiety, all of that desperation. If you use the system and you show them how they can make money, your warm leads can be great. If they're interested, you'll talk; if they're not, you won't waste your breath.

Contacting Your Leads

You can build up a nice basket of leads if you're using all these different avenues to meet people. You've got your Escrow people, seminars, Craigslist, Private Money Pro list, auctions, public records, and family and friends. Next, I'm going to show you the method of how to mail the letter. This is an old school marketing technique that's been around for years and years. Then we'll get into what you actually say.

First, when you mail a letter to anybody you want them to open it. So, you have to make your letter look mysterious. Use a colorful envelope or the big envelope,

8 ½ by 11. Everybody opens the big ones first. Next, use a lady's handwriting if you can. If you're not a lady and you don't have access to a lady who will write these for you, go ahead and use your own handwriting. Handwritten looks way better than something printed. Third, just put the return address; you don't need a name. Or, use your last name only because it can look more personal that way. Four, use a live stamp, meaning one that you actually lick.

The whole purpose is you want them to open the letter. We want them to open this letter so you can introduce yourself to them and create a relationship. You can be telling them, "Hey, this is what I do. This is what my business is about. I've used private lenders in the past."

You're going to find that they'll say, "Wait, how do I get involved?" The more you can get somebody to chase you as opposed to you chasing them, the higher your success rate will be in raising private money.

This letter introduction is definitely how you're going to want to approach your leads and introduce yourself. They might not all have money to lend right now, so don't be the person who stomps your foot and says, "I got to have money right now!" Get rid of that desperation and that neediness. Be that person who says, "Whenever you want to lend, we'll talk." Stay in touch.

Drip market them letting them know what you've got going on, what you're doing.

Private Money Is Everywhere

When you're armed with your confidence, your credibility, and your contacts you'll find that money is all around you, whether you meet investors on the plane or in the market.

Action Steps

- Go to the places I've mentioned in this chapter. Call an escrow agent, find a seminar, go to a conference, join a real estate club, attend a Meetup group. Go and see what's happening. Look around, see who the movers and shakers are.

- Jump on Craigslist. Type your ad in and look at other ads. See who calls. Your confidence will continue to grow as you listen and apply what I teach.

- Start to take action and you will begin to see the results of your labor.

CHAPTER 2

CREDIBILITY

I taught a new investor exactly how to build a credibility package not based on where they worked, what college they attended, or even what they'd personally done. Instead, we build it around the projects that had already been done in their area to show proof of concept.

One of my clients built it exactly the way I showed them. Though this client had never done a deal before, they walked into a meeting with a seasoned private investor and presented the packet. When this private investor looked at her packet, he thought, "Wow, you know how to find the good deals. You know the people who can bring this thing to fruition. You clearly know the players and the pieces of this game. If you can produce the same type of results you show here, I would rather work with you than some of my other seasoned partners who are a little bit sloppier when it comes to putting in everything together."

When you present a concise way of showing your credibility, investors love to do a deal with you. Having a clean credibility package will give you the confidence to walk in and show numbers, show proof of concept. It's not something jotted down on the back of a napkin. It's real data: "In the last 30, 60, or 90 days, this is what's been done."

My client asked the investor the question, "If I can bring you a deal like this, would you want to invest in it?" Of course, the answer is, "Absolutely."

When you build your credibility package the way I teach, experiences like this will happen to you often. In this chapter, we dive into building your credibility. I've heard from so many private money lenders who say, "I don't even know who the heck this person is, and now they are asking for a loan. I wish they would tell me who they are."

Create Your Bio

You need to come up with a bio that's compelling and relatable. You may think to yourself, "I don't have anything great about my bio." Nonsense. What have you done? Give them a little peek, a snapshot, or a portrait of who you are and of what kind of person you are. Maybe you've had a great job or accomplishment. Maybe you've received some sort of honor or an award. They may not be accomplishments in the real estate world, but it is important to convey that you are an accomplished person. This part of your bio is all about showing you have some sort of credibility, that you are a smart individual. That you have done something noteworthy.

For example, I saw one woman say, "I'm a single mom of three kids and I've raised those kids to be amazing people. If I can raise three kids on my own, I can certainly handle a real estate deal. Let's go." She raised a lot of money that way. It was her claim to fame.

In seminars, I've seen people wear a sign around their neck that says, "Great credit, but I have no cash. Looking for joint venture partners." Because they let their ego go, they get results. You've probably heard, "Your ego is not your amigo." The people with the signs are saying, "I'm not where I want to be, so I'm looking for help along the way."

Your bio can contain anything you want. If somebody has ever said to you, "Wow, you're really good at X, or you're amazing at Y, or that's so cool," you want to put it in a great little bio. Position yourself as reliable, trustworthy, a go-getter who is driven and passionate about what you do. Because these are attractive qualities. Your credibility is just a part of who you are.

They're handing you cash, so you want a private money investor to look at you and say, "That's the kind of person I want to do business with. That's the kind of person I want to lend money to. Because I know they're going to be driven about it. They're going to be passionate about it. They're going to be reliable. They're going to be trustworthy. When they say something, I know that's the way it's going to happen."

Whether you're dealing with hard money, a private investor, or a private equity fund, the person pulling the trigger is going to be a *person*. Even if you think it's a big institution, it all comes down to a person. And if that individual knows you were an engineer for quite some time, or you received an award for being conscientious about x, y, and z, that shows who you are as a person.

Your Credibility Package

If you have done deals in the past, build a credibility package. I've heard people call it a brag book or a past deals packet. It's a portfolio that shows what you've done. Include a simple before and after page for each of your deals and include both photos and written descriptions for each property. Those words and those pictures are so powerful. Put the address at the top of the page for each deal.

If you've done lots of deals, pick out three and say, "These are three of the 20 deals I've done or three of the 50 deals I've done." Instead of trying to include all of your deals, stick with three and do more before and after pictures. People seem to like pictures. They love to see the transformation. When they see the transformation, what they're thinking in their mind is you were the creator of that huge improvement. They transfer that good feeling they get looking at the photos right onto you: "Wow, look what this person created!"

Next, put the numbers together for the investor to see. Have the address of the property at the top, then put very simple information on the page: purchase price, the rehab budget, your closing costs, the sales price, the profit. Include the timeframe for each deal. How long did it take you to rehab? How long was the property on the market? Whatever it was, be honest.

Finally, state the return on investment, ROI, in percentage terms. That's what any private money investor wants to see. Any investor is thinking, what is my return on my investment going to be? If you tell somebody, "Hey, you can make $50,000 on this deal," what does that mean? If a guy's investing $50,000 and he's making $50,000, that's an amazing return. If the guy's investing $1 million and he's making $50,000, that's not so hot. Everything is contextual. They want to know what that ROI is.

Then, include references: other private money lenders that you have used. Will all of them agree to say something about you? Maybe not, but it all depends on how you ask them. If you say, "I'm building my real estate business and you and I have had a profitable relationship together. I'm going to be raising some more private money for other deals that I'd like to be doing. Would you mind saying something nice about me if somebody calls you?" Or you can ask them to send you something you can quote, such as, "It was a pleasure to work with ____. I made X return on my money." This is called third-party edification or verification.

Do you notice how I always tell you about what my other clients are doing and what they've done? It's because having been on your side of the lens, watching somebody like myself, I would think, "I wonder if I can do that. I wonder if that's something that I can accomplish." I think I can, but then when I hear about somebody else doing it—some normal Joe who has gone from no money to raising millions of dollars or even hundreds of thousands of dollars—it feels more real. I start to think, "If they can do it, I can do it."

References are a testimonial for your business. Get references with contact information.

You're positioning yourself as credible, passionate, driven, reliable, and trustworthy. You want that credibility being pushed right over onto you so it makes them feel calm and reassured, as in, "This is what's going to happen." The reason people do business with you is that they like you and they trust you. This has become a business cliché, but it is repeated for a reason.

A good credibility package shortens the timeframe between meeting an investor and closing a deal because maybe you don't know these people very long. But they look over your packet and say, "Wow, this is a great bio. I see the before and after pictures, that looks nice. Oh, my gosh, they put the numbers together. They understand how the business works."

There will be some people who are very detailed oriented. They may want to see the details for each deal and proof of those details. For these types of investors, be ready to provide proof such as closing documents, a copy of the profit check. When you're doing your first few deals, have them send you a check. It's great for your ability to show your credibility and what you've done.

Think about creating your own YouTube video of what you've done. You can garner a lot of positioning that way and make your bio look even better. If you've done deals and you create a nice business website communicating who you are and what you've done, it adds a lot of credibility to your pitch.

When You Haven't Done Any Deals Yet

Some of you may be saying, "Wait a second. I haven't done any deals. I'm brand new in this business. How do I create credibility?" Let me show you. If you haven't done deals, your credibility packet is going to be very, very similar to if you have done deals, but there's going to be a little twist. Number one, you're still going to put in your bio. Again, you're passionate, you're driven, you're ethical, you're on the move.

Number two, you won't be able to have the before or after pictures and information for your own deals, but you can still create these property sheets using what somebody else has done. You are saying, "I haven't done deals in this area, but I can show you what other investors are doing." This will help you to show proof of concept.

Pick an address of a property that's recently been flipped. Where do you get these addresses? Let's say I want to go into St. Louis. I've never invested there, but I want to be able to create credibility and know that's a great place to invest. If I spent some time on the ground there and go to a real estate club or a conference or jump on Google, Facebook, or LinkedIn, I'll learn about properties in the area that have been successfully flipped.

You're going to have to call a realtor. I use realtors for a host of different reasons: to find contractors, to find past deals, to find investors, or wholesale deals. If you have a realtor in mind you can call that person. If not, call a big box realty store like Keller Williams and say,

"Hey, I would like to connect with the realtor who deals with investors."

I call the realtor, whether it be a big box store or a realtor that I've been recommended by somebody else and I ask them this simple question: "Can you send me three properties that have been flipped in the last 90 days?"

They'll go through the Multiple Listing System, the MLS, and see pictures of stuff that has been redone. Or they can type in keywords such as "recently remodeled," or "rehabbed head to toe." If they ask, "Why do you want to see that?" you say, "I'm new to the area, and I want to begin flipping properties here," or, "I want to be buying rentals and need to see what my competition is doing to their homes."

Say, "Please send me the Agent Full Report." There will be specific information on that report you want to gather. If she asks, "Why do you want the Agent Full Report?" reply, "I'd like to reach out to whoever the realtor is that sold that property and see if they'll give me the information of their contractor."

Once you get the Agent Full Report, at the bottom of the sold listing is the selling realtor information. There's a reason this is good news: you'll talk to that realtor to get information as well as photos. You can find the before and after picture for the property on Redfin, Trulia, Zillow, or get the MLS pics from that realtor.

Before you talk to the selling realtor, ask yourself what information you need:

- purchase price
- rehab cost
- closing costs
- listing price
- sales price

That data will give us our profit number. The realtor is the key. When I call, I say, "My name is Keith. I saw the property you recently sold at _____ address, great job! Also, I'm a real estate investor and I buy properties very similar to the one I notice that you sold at _____ address. I've got a question for you. Did you happen to help them acquire that property as well?" Eight out of ten times, they're going to say, "Yes, I did help them acquire that property." You can get information on the purchase price and the sold price from public records, but they'll probably give it to you.

You say, "Awesome! These are the types of properties I buy as well." You can get on their list. That way if they're good at finding these types of deals, you'll have an ally. Some realtors are great at finding properties, some are amazing at selling properties. Sometimes they're mutually exclusive. One's a real go-getter and has a ton of patience and is okay with putting in tons of offers. Others are selling agents and they just want to sell, sell, sell.

Next, I say, "You know what, that's great. I'm looking for a good contractor in this area, do you happen to know the contractor who did this job?" I have always found them to say "Yes, I do." Ask, "Can I get their contact info?"

Don't be afraid to ask for what you want. They'll give you the contractor's information. Call the contractor. What I like about these realtors and what I like about these contractors is they already understand what we do. They understand we buy stuff that is majorly beat up, we renovate it, and then we sell it off. So, it goes from dumpy and dreary to a diamond that's dazzling.

Call the contractor and say, "Hey, how's it going? My name is Keith. I'm a real estate investor. I saw that you rehabbed the house on such and such street. You did a fabulous job. I look for guys like you. Can you send me over what it cost? Send me over the scope of work so I get a feeling for your pricing and how much you use." If you haven't been through any courses that teach you how to find contractors or find good realtors, this is one of the best ways. The contractor will most likely give you that information because they want to get work. If you show that you are a possible future job for them, they want to give you information.

Now you have the rehab price. Assume that whoever flipped the property used all cash—similar to the cash that you want to use when you're doing your deals. You can punch the information you've gathered into any good profit calculator, and voila: you get the profit number. You have the purchase price, you have the rehab, you punch it in. You know there's going to be a closing cost. It's going to be a percentage of whatever the sold price is. Let's say the sold price times 5% or 6%, depending on how much your realtor charges you to list the property. Then the closing costs are going to be around another 2% on top of the commissions. Add these up: the purchase price plus rehab plus closing costs. Then the sold price minus those expenses gives you your profit. Then, calculate the return-on-investment, ROI, percentage.

To create credibility in this scenario, you have taken what others have done and shown exactly how they did it. You've met a contractor who is now going to be a part of your team. You're creating credibility by talking with a realtor who is now on your team as well. Those are the people you're going to deal with more than anybody. Realtors in helping you buy and sell property, and the contractors helping you fix that property up.

For each deal you've researched, you've got a before and after picture. This isn't your job; this isn't your deal. That's okay. When you present this to a private money investor, you say, "This is our competition's deal. This is what's been going on."

If you can show three in the area and you have a full book of them, you are saying, "Look at the proof of concept. I'm not just pulling this wild idea out of my head that I think I can go flip a property there." You're saying, "I understand I can go flip property there. Others have been doing it and I have a realtor and a contractor who are familiar with this model. They have experience in this market." The experience that they have is now being transferred on to you because you put together the research.

What this conveys to the private lender is you know the right process, you know the right people and you know what deals will make good profit.

Once you have showed this credibility package to them you need to ask them one question: "If I bring you a deal like one of these, would you invest with me?"

That is the point of this whole thing, to be able to ask that one question. This way when they say "Yes!" you know exactly who to bring your next deal to J

If I told you I was hanging out with my friend Goldie who is on the TV show *Sons of Anarchy*, you'd look at me differently. It's like his celebrity status somehow got transferred onto me in your eyes. You're doing the same thing here. You say, "This realtor and this contractor, they're well known in the area. They've done deals. Here are a few that they've been a part of." It shows that you have established yourself wide and deep in that area—that you know who to talk to. You know how to research and branch out and meet with people who have had success in that area. All their success transfers onto you. This is how you will create a credibility booklet of deals.

Even using someone else's deals, you can still provide references. At this point, because you are new, these are going to be character references. They should convey that you're not the kind of person who walks away when things get tough. You're not the person that's just going to lay down because you're afraid of a little hard work. Present a character reference that says, "This guy does a good job."

Putting It All Together

These elements all layer right on top of each other. Present an amazing, content-rich investor packet (I'll show you this later in the book). You might want to call it a deal proposal. "Here's my bio, here's my credibility booklet. These are the things that have been done in that area so I know it's doable. Here are my character references, and by the way, here's my content-rich investor packet."

When you have all these stacked together, your credibility looks solid.

If you're one of these investors that just sends in comps, you look sloppy. Nobody enjoys sloppy, not when you're doing business together. Not when you're investing big chunks of money together.

I hope after reading this, you can feel like you've got something to offer: a good bio, a good character, good research skills. Are you reliable and driven? If you've researched an area and found all the information you need to show what other people are doing, if you have good character references from people that know you, and put it all together with a content-rich packet, all these layers stacked together will show a lender you aren't a big risk.

That's how you build credibility in a major way, even if you've never done deals.

Action Steps

- Put real effort into writing your bio. What rewards have you received? What honor have you earned? What have your friends said about you? What makes you unique? What is your unique selling position to the market of investors and why they would want to invest with you? Keep it one paragraph max. Simple is better.

- Build a credibility packet based on your own deals or based on the deals that others have done in the area you are wanting to invest.

CHAPTER 3

CONTENT

Not too long ago, I had a client come to me and who was ecstatic—just thrilled. She said, "Keith, you're not going to believe what happened to me."

I thought, "I've been around the block a time or two. I doubt whatever she says will shock me."

Then, she said, "I built the content package—the investor packet—exactly the way you showed me to. It included the executive summary, details, pictures, comp, and renovation. I built it all out and took it to a real estate investment group meeting. I presented it to the president and said, 'Hey, do you mind if I stand up and present this deal to the group?'"

She told me the president grabbed the packet, thumbed through it, and said, "You cannot present this to the group."

Shocked, she asked, "Why not?"

He said, "Because this deal is so good, I want to fund it and I don't want anybody else to have the opportunity."

She said, "That's fantastic! You can fund this deal, but do you mind if I present? That way when I bring more deals like this, I'll have other investors ready?"

He said, "No problem. But promise me I get this deal." She said, "You bet."

That's what happens when you build the content in the right way and put it in front of the right person. These are the types of results you will get.

Now that you figured out how to build your credibility whether you've done deals or not, the next piece of the private money puzzle is the second C: having great content. Content refers to the information that you're giving a potential private money investor. It should be clear and concise.

Your content helps the investor understand where you're going with their investment. I am going to show you how to build an investor packet. This can also be called a presentation packet, a property presentation packet, an executive summary, a deal flow packet, or a deal packet. I don't care what you call it as long as you have all the content in the right place. Your goal is to provide information in such a way that the investor reviewing it thinks, "Whoa, that's a good deal. I want to get on top of it."

Executive Summary

First, you need an executive summary. This is a short summary of exactly what's going on. They're not looking for an encyclopedia of real estate terms and jargon. They're simply looking to get to the point: how much money can we make? Start by providing the property address and the specifications of the property: the bed, bath mix, the year built, square footage, the purchase price, the rehab budget, the After Repair Value (ARV): how much you can sell the property for, the projected profit, and the ROI. Whenever you dealing with investors, give them an exit strategy. Are you going to flip for a very big chunk of cash or are you going to hold on for long term profit? Next, give them your contact information. Finally, tell them what the days on the market typically are for that area.

This whole thing is going to be laid out in paragraph format:

I've got a property located at 123 Main Street. It's a three-bedroom, two-bath, house built in 1984, with 1500 square feet. We are buying the property for $110,000. The rehab budget is going to be $30,000. The ARV is going to be $190,000. The projected profit is going to be $32,000, a 21 percent ROI for the deal. Our exit strategy is to flip this for a chunk of cash. Our contact info is _____. The *days on the market for others in this area: around 30 days or less. So, we expect this project to take four to six months.*

When you give the address, you might also want to mention you know something about the area. It may be a really hot area; it may be an awesome area for a specific reason. Make note of that so the person reading thinks, "Oh wow, that's a great area. I want to be investing in that neighborhood."

Proof

How are you going to prove the specifications of the address? It's very simple. You include the listing. If the property is from a wholesaler and isn't on the MLS, you can get a tax record. This will also have important information about the address and specifications. Provide the assessor's record. If you happen to have the purchase agreement, include it. But as soon as you get a verbal acceptance on the deal, you're going to be putting this package together. So, you may not have the written purchase agreement back yet and that's okay. Include that later.

Next, offer some documentation regarding your rehab budget. Include the rehab bid you're your contractor. And you can put in bids from three different contractors if you don't have a guy that you are already working with. Putting this content together is what separates the hobbyist from the pros.

Photos

Next, include pictures of the property. You can get these from the real estate websites: Zillow, Redfin, etc.

ARV and Projected Profit

Show what your ARV and projected profit is. How? Show comps, otherwise known as comparable property sales. Include three if you can. In a hot market, you may only have one or two. That's okay. But include what you can. Comps will prove the number of days on the market you can expect, what your exit strategy is, what your ARV will be, and what kind of projected profit you might want to use.

I put in a simple-to-follow profit breakdown. It is very similar to the credibility sheet: here is our purchase price, here's our rehab budget, here's what the closing cost going to be. Here what we believe we are going to sell it for, and here's our projected estimated profit. It doesn't have to be super complicated.

When you are dealing with a private investor and/ or hard money lender and actually go to close, you're going to use a mortgage or deed of trust and a promissory note. Sometimes you will use some different kinds of documents. Here's a list of docs you might need: a deed of trust or mortgage, a promissory note, a joint venture agreement. Put everything in writing. That way, we don't have to have a good memory. Putting everything in writing defines roles so everybody knows what they're supposed to be doing and nobody forgets what is supposed to be done.

This type of information is backing up what you're telling potential investors in your story. Every good story should have proof.

How to Get Your Information

Get the listing from a realtor. That's pretty simple. Your rehab budget you get from your contractors. You can pull property photos off of Redfin, Trulia, Zillow. The comps, you're going to get that from your realtor. Your simple to follow profit break down? You can create that. It's a very simple one-sheet.

To download templates for the deed of trust, the mortgage, promissory note, or joint venture agreement, go to www.privatemoneysecretsbook.com Of course, different states have different standard documents. So, get a hold of your closing attorney in whatever state you're in. Or, call the escrow company. They can draft you a deed of trust, a mortgage, a promissory note, a balloon note, a real estate lien, whatever you may require. A joint venture agreement you can grab from our resource guide. Run it past your attorney make sure that she likes it.

How to Organize Your Content

On the first page, put a picture of the property and the address at the top. Next, include a line that says, "Offered by" and then you put your company information right here. Make it look good. If you're not tech-savvy, join the club. I hired somebody for $25 an hour and had them create a template. That way I can look more professional. In every aspect of your business, you want to be excellent.

On the second page, you have the executive summary: a paragraph and some very simple bullet points, the property specs. Next, include a page of photos. Six pictures are perfect, it doesn't have to be anything too exhaustive or crazy. Gives them a good idea of kind of what's happening.

On page four, include a rehab bid or bids with line items. Go ahead and include actual estimates. Make a note to always account for a ten to fifteen percent over. It's just the way it is. There's going to be a change or they are going to open up a wall and find termites. This kind of note shows you are savvy, you get it. Take my word for it and add 15 percent on top of your bids to get a realistic rehab budget.

Next, attach the listing or tax sheet. Then you want to have the comps page. If I am going to provide three comps, I'll put a picture for each comp and put all the specs off to the right. Including the proximity to your property is nice. The comps page should say when each property sold, for how much it sold for. Include a map of your comps from Google, Apple, or Bing. It shows that truly the comps are where you say they are. Maps help investors get a good feeling for what's going on. If you don't know how to create and print a comps map, talk to techie person and they'll show you.

Finally, present the breakdown of profit. I can't emphasize enough to always be thinking in terms of ROI and what a real investor is wanting to make. If you happen to be using a joint venture, an LLC together, put the operating agreement in this packet. Put a mortgage and note together and include it. If you happen to have it, include the purchase agreement. If you don't have it yet, write "purchase agreement to follow." It means that you know what you're doing. Another good thing to include is the preliminary title report. If you don't have it yet, write "the preliminary title report to follow."

Let's review. The executive summary exists to grab an investor and help them say, "Yes, I want to do this deal. This sounds interesting. It looks profitable. I'm in." Then they go over to the pictures page. Next, they look at the estimate and rehab bids. Then, there's the listing and tax sheet. It shows them that the property does, in fact, have X number of bedrooms, this many baths, et cetera. The comp sheets show an ARV is worth something. You're proving it with this documentation.

You're showing the proximity of the comps to the property right there via a map. You're showing the breakdown of profits so they can see the numbers very clearly as you are laying them out. If you're going to use a joint venture agreement you include a joint venture agreement. If you use a mortgage and note, you put a mortgage and note there. Both are fine. I prefer mortgage and note as a lender. Then you can write either, "the purchase agreement to follow," or "preliminary title report to follow." If you have both of them, then go ahead and include them.

This is the flow of what your investor packet should look like. With this content, you will be looked at as an expert with the opportunity to share. You have the opportunity and are proving it is why you say it is. If you can put it together like this, you are going to do very well.

Understand Your Content

I want to go over with you what certain documents consist of and the relationship between them so you understand exactly how these things work. When you're dealing with any private lender, there will be two documents called security instruments. First is a promissory note, otherwise known as a real estate lien, or a plain old simple note. It is an IOU that says, "I promise to pay you." You have the entities involved. You have the amount of the loan. You have the terms, you have the conditions, you have the interest rate, and any of your default clauses. Then you'll sign. So, again, this note simply identifies:

- Who is involved?
- How much is the loan?
- What are the terms?
- What's the length?
- What are the conditions?
- What's the interest rate?
- What happens if I default? If I stop making the payments what is the legal ramification?

Most of the time, this is a private document because the terms are between you and the person who did the note. It's nobody else's business.

A different type of document is the mortgage. In some states, it is known as the deed of trust. And what this is saying is basically, "I don't trust you." Therefore, we are going to record this and make it a public document. It has a lot of the same information as the promissory note I just explained: the entities, the amount of the loan. It doesn't include the terms, conditions, or the interest rate, but it does have the default clauses in there. Both parties sign. Or you'll be signing and they'll be a notary. It's a public document this is now recorded at the recorder's office. Sometimes, there will be a first mortgage on record and then a second mortgage as well. It would be a senior position versus a junior position. This is the language and the terminology we use. When you understand how this all works, your credibility goes up.

Deal Directly

The people that will prepare the closing documents for you are your escrow agent or a closing attorney. Even if you're savvy and you make an all-cash offer, you still need help. Let's say you are going to use somebody else's private money, a hard money loan, and a little bit of your own cash so you can leverage yourself and do more deals. Deal with the escrow agent or the closing attorney directly.

Bypass your real estate agent. Real estate agents, I love them, I use them a lot and think they're great, but many times, they don't understand how a lot of this works. So, I want to be the point contact when I am dealing with the escrow agent and the closing attorney. I am paying for their services, not the real estate agent. So, I'd rather deal with them directly, and send in the documentation three or four days before a property is supposed to close. Once you find out who these effective closing attorneys or escrow agents are, you can send them a mailer and develop a relationship.

This way, you can make changes: "Listen, we are changing this to a hard money loan. I'm using my cash for something else. I decided to use a hard money loan." That's all you need to do when you deal directly with the closing attorney. Real estate agents will freak out when you want to make changes, but escrow agents or closing attorneys will not. You can simply say, "Prepare this note, prepare this deed. Prepare this mortgage." These get recorded.

The Sequence of a Deal

I get a lot of private investors who come to me to learn how to structure the deal better. It is helpful to understand how the paperwork goes together, how is it sequenced. That's something that you need to know and that's something you need to understand so you're not taken by surprise.

First, you get the deal accepted. Your intent to buy is accepted. As soon as you get that deal accepted, that is when we go into what I like to call FBI Mode. You're checking all your facts, your figures. You are making sure everything is good. You're going to check your comps to make sure your ARV is spot on. Google map the area and do a 360-degree view. Get the contractors' bids. Gather property photos.

Call three realtors and ask them a very simple question: "I'm about to buy this property and fix it up and relist it but I'm not sure whom I am going to list it with. If I was to list it with you, how much do you think I should list it for after I renovate it? Tell me why." Ask, "Can you tell me if there's something about the neighbor I need know?" If you are investing remotely, you need to know these types of things. So, I call realtors and I want them to confirm to me what they think the ARV should be.

I am investigating what's happening, and I build an investor packet. Here is when you have your due diligence period, seven to ten days of due diligence and research. Somewhere in there, you have to put some earnest money down—deposit money. If you have your lender already lined up beforehand, they can be the one who puts in the earnest money deposit. You get all of this lined up before. If you don't have any lender for your deal, you have seven to ten days to be lining all of this up after you get your verbal acceptance. There's a little gray area here. The time between when you get the verbal acceptance and the written one. Use that time wisely. Sometimes it's only a day or two.

Then, I send it out to investors at all the spots I showed you. I send that packet to everybody all at once. I am looking for people to commit. If I say I am all cash; I made an offer all cash but right before the closing it turns out I am coming in with a mixture of hard money lenders or private lenders? What I do is I send in mortgage docs directly to the closing attorney or to the escrow agent. That way, everything's good to go. As soon as you get accepted, verify, verify, verify. Then you build an investor pack. You send out the investor packs to all these contacts all at the same time. See who's interested. You want people to be interested even after the deal is gone.

This is what happens. You're always raising money and looking for deals. Those are the things you do in this business. Raise money, look for deals, and manage contractors. That's it, three things. This is the sequence; this is the timeline. Understand it. Don't freak out. Know that your escrow lady and your closing attorney understand this timeline. So even if you're not an expert at it, they are.

Action Steps

- Call up an escrow agent or a closing attorney and ask them to send you an example of a mortgage, a deed of trust, a note, and a joint venture agreement that they have seen that is effective. Get familiar with what those documents look like in your state.
- Take a deal, any deal, and create an investor packet as if you're going to present it to somebody you've met at a seminar.

These exercises are going to show you what practical questions you will encounter in the field so you'll know how to address them. You will then be all set to rock 'n roll when investors are lined up and you're ready to take action. Want to see the questions I ask? Go to www. privatemoneysecretsbook.com and I'll show you.

CONFIDENCE

Confidence is one of the most attractive character traits or qualities of any human being. Whether you're male or female, confidence is crucial. So, when you're meeting with investors, you need to be sure your confidence is soaring. The way to project massive confidence is by knowing you are credible: that you have the right content. Belief in who you are and what you do is the most important thing there is in this business.

I recently brought a deal to a private investor. He looked at the comps and said, "I can see where you're going with this. I kind of agree that the ARV is exactly what you say, but I'm going to lean on you. Do you believe that you can make this happen? Do you believe the ARV is what you say it is?"

The decision was in my hands. The question of whether he was going to invest was based solely on whether I believed we could make this deal work—if my numbers were truly accurate.

Yes, investors are going to look at numbers. But at some point, they're simply going to look you in the eye and ask, "Do you believe we can make this happen?" That's why it's so important to have a high level of confidence.

Get it, guard it, grow it. That's what I will explain in this chapter.

You know 1) where to connect with private money people, 2) how to build your credibility whether you've done deals or not, and 3) how to put together the right content. The next piece is to have confidence: to understand the mindset required to attract private money investors. There are a few principles I want to go over with you here that are worth noting. These principles are going to serve you well in your business.

Focus

First, stay focused on one thing. If you come in and you talk to a possible investor and you say, "I'm going to do some single-family residences and then I'm going to maybe do some apartment buildings. I'm also interested in raw land deals and I absolutely love commercial products," you're going to fail because you're all over the board. My wheelhouse has been single-family residences.

From there, I built my investors up to doing multi-family units.

Stay focused. If you come in and announce you are doing everything, they're going to know you're an expert at nothing. It will be tempting to do deals on a lot of different types of properties. There's a lot of shiny stuff out there. But an old business partner of mine said, "Don't chase the shiny stuff." Instead, be singularly focused on what you do so you become the expert at exactly that.

Discomfort

If something you're doing is uncomfortable—and I know that this new skill is uncomfortable—that means you are experiencing growth. You are increasing in maturity. Succeeding in real estate was not easy for any of us, so don't expect it to be easy for you. Because there are so many negative taboos or negative connotations regarding money (particularly raising money or borrowing money), it is easy to get uncomfortable and to want to stop growing. But these are thoughts that we have to eliminate or switch in our brain.

If you are uncomfortable, please know you're not alone. A lot of us have been uncomfortable raising private money at the beginning. Our mindset had to shift. We had to realize that we were not *borrowing* money

necessarily, but giving somebody the opportunity to
make money. That's the key shift here.

Momentum and Competence

The last thing I want to mention is momentum makes
this easier. As you start to build momentum in your
business, you're finding deals. You now know how to
make yourself look credible and you're stacking that on
top with good content. These two things alone are going
to cause you to be a lot more confident.

The reason why people lack confidence—and there
have been lots of psychological studies on this that I
don't want to bore you with—is they lack competence. I
love studying why people do what they do. Why do we
think the way we think? Why is our behavior mapped
out a certain way? A lot of psychologists have boiled it
down and found that confidence is directly linked to
competence.

Let me give you an example. I have a nearly 16-year-
old son. We go out on these drives because he's got his
driver's permit and I'm teaching him how to drive. Every
move he makes as a new driver is super-calculated, from
the switching on of the blinker, to the shifting of the car
into reverse, to the looking over the shoulder, to backing
up, to parking, to getting onto the freeway. Since all of
those moves are new, he's uncomfortable. He knows he

is unskilled and he's not very competent. But wasn't that all of us when we got behind the wheel for the very first time? It was.

When you get into these situations and you're looking to raise private money, you'll feel like a new driver. You've built your credibility packet. You've built your investor packet. You have your content filled. You're going to lack a little bit of confidence only because your competency isn't there yet. It's okay.

Let me tell you something that might happen. They call me the "realest guy in real estate" for a reason. You may go and try and fund your first deal and it may fall through. Rather than looking at that as a failure, I want you to look at that as feedback. You got a lot closer than those who never pursued the deal at all. You'll push yourself further and further and further until eventually, it's going to pop. Just don't lose heart. Keep sowing and you're going to reap. Trust me.

By understanding that confidence is linked to competence, you'll do well. The very fact that you are reading this book is a good sign. Studying and joining my coaching group will elevate your confidence. These are all things that are building your competency, and therefore, your confidence. As you come to know the terms and all of the words you should be using when you're talking to a potential investor about your deal, your confidence will grow. When you actually have numbers that work, you will be confident in how you present.

Negative Beliefs

There are some demons that we all meet from time to time. Thoughts like, "I'm not good enough," "This is hard," or, "Nobody wants to listen to me." We've got to get rid of some of the negative mindset. To help you, I'm going to list some very common negative mindsets and how we can alter them. I see hang-ups about money, as well as many negative beliefs about borrowing or using good debt.

First of all, you don't want to approach anybody because you feel like maybe you are a bother. The truth of the matter is, yes you are a bother to somebody who doesn't want to lend you money. But you're not a bother at all to somebody that wants to give you money. The way to get over this, "I'm a bother" idea is to remember what you are giving somebody. You are giving them an opportunity. It's the antithesis of a bother.

If you had money to give to somebody, would you say, "I don't want to bother them by giving them money?" No, you'd be like, "I know I'm not a bother because I'm going to give you money." You're giving them an opportunity. This has to be your mindset. It has to be how you feel about your opportunity. It's how you have to feel about the real estate deal that you're getting into. If you feel like, "Wow, this is an opportunity for you," then you're going to approach a potential investor with a lot more confidence than if you carry around the idea of, "I hate to bother." It will come across in your physiology 100%.

The next thing that you have to get over is the idea of, "I am a beggar." Do not beg for money. Unless you live on the side of the freeway and have a cardboard sign in your hand, do not beg for money. Somebody who is successful, who is doing real estate deals, does not need to beg for money. The reason you're not going to be a beggar is that you're going to have the mindset that says there are lots and lots of people who want to invest.

The way to destroy demons in your brain is to combat them with the truth. That's just the way it is. If you think you're a bother or a beggar, switch it with truth: "I'm giving them an opportunity. There are lots and lots of people who want to invest." You don't have to go to one person and think you have to beg them for money. That's not the way it works. That thought flows from a small or scarce mentality that holds there are only a few people out there who want to give you money to do your deals. No way. There's a ton.

There's a lot of people out there. If somebody says no, say to yourself, "Next!" I'm going to show you the phraseology in the closing chapter on how to get investors to chase you as opposed to you chasing them. It's psychology. "I don't want to be a bother." "I don't want to be a beggar." These are the types of negative thoughts that will sink you. Get rid of them.

Another one I've seen is, "Raising money is hard." A lot of people hold that belief, but it is not hard to raise money if you have a good deal, great credibility, and excellent content to show the investor. You have to go to where these people happen to be. I showed you earlier where to connect with everybody. If you know where private money investors are hanging out and you know what they're interested in, do you feel like fishing is so hard? No. If you know there's fish there and you know what they're eating, you'll catch one. You drop the bait down at the right time of the day and now, it's fun. It's exciting.

This is the mentality you have to have. Instead of telling yourself that raising money is hard, tell yourself that raising money is fun. It's easy. I don't care who you are, how many millions of dollars you've raised. I've raised more than pretty much anybody I've ever met, and I still think it's very fun.

When I first started, I used to have to, literally, go for a drive in my truck and tell myself over and over that raising private money is fun: "I love raising private money. I love the challenge of raising private money. I'm great at raising private money. People want to invest with me because my deals are amazing."

You have this loop in your brain and you need to make sure it is repeating helpful messages. Your subconscious believes anything you tell it. If you tell it, "I'm a loser. I suck at raising private money. I'm horrible," your subconscious is going to believe it. I don't even say it. I interrupt that pattern. If I accidentally think, "Raising money is hard," I immediately interrupt myself with, "Absolutely not. Raising private money is easy. It's what I love to do. It's fun. I'm going fishing. It's fun."

Types of Debt

Next up in the litany of negative beliefs I've often seen is, "Debt is bad." No. The truth is *bad* debt is bad. Good debt is good. If you are borrowing money to make more money, that's good debt. If you take out a loan for a million dollars and buy a piece of property that's worth a million-two or a million-three and it costs you $7,000 a month to make that payment, yet you're bringing in $13,000 a month and you're positive cash flowing, that original loan is great! When it's all said and done, you're in the black, month after month. For ease of numbers, let's say you're clearing $6,000. You have to pay $7,000 but you're making $6,000. Is that original debt a good thing or a bad thing? It's obviously a great thing.

"Debt is bad." Not true. Bad debt is bad. Good debt is great. If you use debt to buy things that you are only going to consume, then it's a liability. You want to be careful about that kind of debt. You do not need credit cards to buy nonsense. Excess or lavish living expenses that never pay you back are not good. But if you're spending money to invest in an asset that is making you money, that's good debt.

There are two types of good debt: investing in something that's going to pay you back and investing in your education. Because when you invest in your education, you are now gaining knowledge to make you more money. In all actuality you are investing in YOU. YOU are your greatest asset. You will create more money than any other thing you own or control. Remember when you invest in your education you are investing in upgrading you and the way you think. There is no greater investment than that.

Just recently, I hired a mentor to teach me certain things. Even at this point in my career, having raised close to $50 million dollars in the last 12 years, I still hire coaches and I still hire mentors. I still mastermind with people who have gone further than me in the industry that I am interested in.

I'm always gobbling up content, whatever I can find that's going to help me make more money or help me enjoy my life more. I'm interested in—and willing to pay for—any kind of knowledge that is going to make my life easier, or going to get me from point A to point B faster and with less pain. Sign me up. I'm at live events all the time. I'm at conferences all the time. These seminars cause me to grow and grow. My competence goes through the roof; therefore, my confidence goes through the roof.

Experience

The other thing I hear a lot from my students is, "I lack experience." Well, guess what. I also lacked experience when I got started, and so did a lot of people. You're going to combat that negative thought with the truth: "I am credible because of what I laid out here and what I've learned. I have good content. These are two things that I have. Where I may lack experience, I am giving them a great opportunity. It's going to make them money. Therefore, who cares if I lack experience."

You can leverage other people's experiences and learn from them. Yes, you have to have good content. You have to have a good deal. If you are credible, you will be able to say, "Even though I lack experience, I'm going to show you a good deal."

Hard money lenders and private money lenders are going to lend on what? They're going to lend on the deal. So, if they see that there's a great opportunity, then they're going to be saying, "I'm interested. I believe in you because your credibility package is terrific. You showed me that you are passionate, honest, trustworthy, and driven. When you showed me the content package, I realized this deal has an 18% ROI. There are reasons why you'll be able to sell it. We'll be able to do what we need to do. I'm secure because you put the proper documentation in place."

"I lack experience." Hogwash. Replace that thought with: "I'm credible and I've got good content."

There's nothing different between you and me. I walk around very confident that I can raise cash for real estate deals because I've done a lot of it. But you can walk around with that same confidence too if you do exactly what I explain in this book. Momentum makes things easier and easier. Later will eventually become now. If you are investing for here and now, and you're building a track record, you'll be in business for a while. Your credibility will continue to grow. You'll have deals that you've done. You'll continue to get cheaper money and more money. Lots of things will be happening that will be making people excited to invest in you.

This person that you're talking to now may not invest until later. Don't ruin that lead by trying to close them right now. This idea of, "Oh my gosh, I got to do it now, now, now?" No. You throw out your opportunities if you're too high-pressure. Be relaxed. Because when later comes, they'll be all warm and ready to go. You're taking them through a process of how they get to learn and how they get to become a part of this opportunity. Be long-term minded. Yes, stuff needs to happen now, but it can also happen later.

Now, let's get into the mindset of a lender. When you know exactly what they're thinking, you know exactly what to give them.

Understanding the Lender Mindset

Here's how the system works: You've got the property and you've got the lender, whether that is a bank, financial institution, or private investor. You make the payment to the lender and that lender has the property itself for security. Meaning if you default on your payment, they get to keep the property. The property is for you to use, whether you're going to live in it or use it as an investment vehicle by fixing it up and flipping it for profit or by renting it out.

This is the circle of lending. You make your payment, they make sure the house stays with you, you get to use the house, and everybody's happy. But how do they make their money? Let me break it down for you.

Three Pools of Money

A lender is either a broker or a private investor. If he's a broker, there are two ways that he has money. First: he has put together a whole pool of people. Each one of these people represents a dollar amount. Maybe $50,000. Maybe $75,000. The broker acts as an underwriter for the group. He'll match up your deal with the right investor or group of investors and put that money to work. The second way the broker has access to money is something I call the giant credit card. Or a warehouse line of credit. He is borrowing this money at a certain percentage. Anywhere from six to eight percent, generally. This large facility or warehouse line of credit is made available if that broker can get the right collateral.

A private investor simply has his own money that he can offer to you. These are the three scenarios. If he's a broker, then he's coming from a facility or he has a pool of investors. If he's his own private investor, he has his own money.

Here is an example: your deal consists of a 3/2, 1500 sq. ft., built in 1981. You need $80,000 to purchase. You need $20,000 for rehab and the ARV is worth, let's say, $160,000. You bring this deal to him and say, "I've got this 3/2, 1500 sq. ft., built in 1981. I'm going to buy it for $80,000, stick $20,000 into it and I'm going to sell this thing for $160,000."

He would look at that deal and say, "Okay, that meets my parameters."

His parameters might be that the investment is 65% of the after-repair value, 80% of the purchase price because they want to see some of your own skin in the game. Or, if it's a private investor and he puts up the entire thing, he wants to joint venture with you for 50/50 percent of the profit. Or, maybe he wants to make 12% annually on his money. If you flip it two times, you're getting the best deal ever. There's a whole host of different scenarios.

The broker, if he's doing a deal for others, or the investor who is simply doing a deal for himself, must look at your deal and size it up. Ultimately, he needs to be the underwriter. Underwriting means weighing the risk to reward ratio: "Should I put the money out? Is there a big risk here? Am I safe? How am I safe?"

If he likes the parameters of what you offer, the broker can then deal with the people who have $160,000 or two people who each have $80,000. In this case, the broker puts two different people on the deed of trust. It's a split deed of trust. This arrangement is very common amongst these pool investors. The broker would underwrite the deal, put you through escrow, and put you in touch with the investors funding the deal.

If it's his own money, he's going to look at it and say, "I'm going to go ahead and do the deal."

Or if he has a big facility, he's probably having to meet with a board of advisors who decide whether they want to do that deal or not. Regardless, it's all human interaction. Know that it's all human interaction even if you're having to upload the pertinent details of a deal via a website or an app. Those are simply filtering systems to get to the good deals. It's still going to be a human being that determines whether or not someone funds the deal or not. That's why credibility and content are so important.

How Brokers Make Money

Brokers routinely put out two advertisements. One says, "Need money?" With this ad, he's reaching out to people like us who need funds for deals. The second ad says, "Make 12% per annum, secured." With that ad, the broker is collecting pools of investors wanting to make 12% on their money. You respond to an ad, bring a deal in, and he underwrites it. He says, "This is perfect. It's what I like."

But how does he make his money? That's what everybody is always asking: How does a hard money guy make his money? First, he makes it off of points. A lot of private people charge points, too. Also known as origination points, points are a percentage of the loan. So, if it's a $100,000 loan and they charge two points, they're going to get $2,000 just to originate the loan. Often, the broker is the one getting the points and interest payments go to the pool of investors. Or at least a portion of the interest payments in some cases.

A broker also makes his money on the difference of interest charged. Let's say he gives his pool of investors 12% and yet charges you 15%. He'll make 3% on that money. Another way that he's going to make money is by servicing the loan. Brokers typically get about half a point to collect the mortgage payment from you, servicing it, putting it in, accounting for it all, and then paying out. That pretty much covers any staff that's taking care of these details.

Finally, there are what I like to call "bologna sauce fees." They're not all bologna sauce, but some of them are. For example, the doc prep fee. Someone is getting $250 for doc prep and they're simply taking a template and changing out three pieces of information. Sometimes, with a hard money lender, they might charge a $395 fee upfront to see if the deal is good. If it goes through, they'll apply that to any of your points paid. That makes sense. But if anybody charges outlandish fees upfront, be very careful. Like in the over $1000 range up front, they are most likely a scam.

There can be a big range on origination points charged, from one point up to ten points, depending on the lender. The interest rate could be anywhere from 5% to 22%. It depends on who you're dealing with. A lot of private brokers might charge you a point to spend all the time getting it all together. Some might not charge you any points at all, depending on how sophisticated they are. If you're dealing with your warm market: friends, family, whatever, and they're looking to you for guidance, you could get your investment for only 6% or 7% for 30 years.

You have to know who you're dealing with. You're going to deal with people who have already done deals and they're going to be a little bit more competitive with their rates because they know what they've got. Or you might deal with some people who aren't that savvy. They're trusting you and they look to you as the expert. The more credible you are and the more content you give them, the more they're going to want to do business with you.

That's how these guys make money. If they're going to put $10 million on the street, they're going to make about $1 million dollars. The points are where they make a lot of their money, and it behooves them to have that money turning, turning, turning. That's why when you have a six months loan, they want to charge you another point or two to extend it for another 90 days or another 180 days. It's because they know it is costing them for you to keep holding onto that money.

Keeping Money in Play

The only way lenders can make money is by *actually lending money*. They're advertising because they're looking for you. Are you going to feel like you're bothering somebody if they're advertising to try and find you? No way. Do you feel like you're a bother to McDonald's when you go in and buy a burger? No. They spend millions and millions of dollars making you feel like you want their burger. They spend money to try and find you and that's what these people—lenders—are doing. Even private investors do this. I know quite a few private investors who are always saying, "I don't want my money on the sidelines, I want it in play. If it's not playing, it's not making me any more money."

A common mindset I see in the working class and the middle class is that rich people just sit around like Scrooge McDuck. They're swimming on piles of gold. That's not the case. They want their money in play so they can make more money on top of their money.

Understanding the mindset of the lender helps build your confidence. If you know someone is advertising to you, do you feel like you're begging him, or that he doesn't have time for you? No! If you have that mindset of, "I'm giving you an opportunity and I know you want to lend to me," you'll do well. Focus on this thought: "We need each other."

That's why seminars are powerful. You need each other, and they are a chance for you to meet. Let's say, for example, you need $100,000 to get your deal done. A hard money guy says, "I'm only going to give you $80,000. That's it. You have to come in with your own construction money." But you don't have it. So, you have him in the first position, the senior position on the deal. Then you would need to find somebody to fulfill the $20,000. We call it gap funding. You're going to find a private investor to do this. Negotiate with him; tell him exactly what you want to do. If he put in the $20,000, maybe he wants 50/50 of your profit. Maybe 60/40. Maybe he only wants 12% per annum. People say, "How do I structure that?" The answer is: however you *want* to structure it. Whatever you can negotiate is what the deal will look like.

Some of you might be amazing negotiators. You're comfortable with money; you don't have money hang-ups. You understand the opportunity and you show somebody, "I'll give you 12% annum per year if you come in the second position." They're like, "Fabulous, let's go, that's exciting." Others might be new at this, so you offer a 50/50 split. Either way, if you're in the beginning stages, this is what you need to do to get your real estate career going.

Do not be afraid. Make sure you have a good deal and move forward with it. The more of these you do, the better. Even if you make $5,000, $7,000, or $10,000 on your first deal, you'll have more confidence inside of you—because now you've been through the entire system. You will then say to yourself, "I understand how these things work."

The Final Word on Confidence

We now know that confidence is linked to competence. Hopefully, as you read you are getting more competent in deal structuring, what to say, and how to build your credibility. I hope you are also seeing some of the thoughts you need to change, such as, "I'm a beggar," or "I'm a borrower," or "I'm a bother." Change those to something more like, "I'm giving people an opportunity," "I'm giving them hope," or, "I'm giving them something that they can make money with me and we can make it together."

Action Step

- Repeat over and over to yourself that raising private money is easy: "I'm a money-raising machine. Raising money is fun." Start to say that over and over. Do it in the morning when you wake up: "I love raising private money. Raising private money is a blast. Raising private money is fun. I am good at it." Repeat it at lunchtime and do it again at night, a minute each time. As you start to say these sentences to yourself repeatedly, you're going to start to believe them. It's going to give you confidence.

CLOSE

As you can imagine, not everything has worked out perfectly in my investing career. A lot of the things that I teach you in this book are designed to help you avoid some of the pitfalls and mistakes I made. I have plenty of stories that still sting a little bit when I recall them. In several instances, I got verbal commitments, but I could not get the investor to wire the money in time. I realized it was my fault entirely. This one particular deal had a lot of juicy profit in it, and I recognized that when I was dealing with the investor, I didn't state exactly what I needed to have happen and when. I was a little bit wishy-washy. I was not altogether confident that he would want to work together. He had felt a little uneasiness, and therefore, the deal fell through.

Yes, I lacked confidence, but it was also the ability to be straightforward, upfront, and simply say, "This is the amount of money we need to do the deal. This is how long it's going to be out. This is how much you're going to make, and this is the day of close. We need the money to be wired in a day early so that we don't have to postpone the closing."

Your ability to close is directly proportionate to how directly and clearly you communicate with an investor. In the deal I just mentioned, I was a little bit hesitant. I thought that by being timid, I would be able to make sure the investor felt comfortable about doing the deal. In reality, it was my hesitation that made him pull back a little bit. While he gave me the verbal approval of the deal, he ended up not actually following through. I lost that deal because I didn't understand how to get investors to close, and that's why we're going to discuss this topic now.

In this chapter, we will cover how to truly close the deal.

There is something that you need to understand. Private investors only need to know three things. How much do you need? How much will I make? And how long will it take? Answer those three things with confidence and you will get more yesses than nos.

We've now covered many important topics. We've talked about where we connect with investors and the best places to meet them. We've discussed how to build up your credibility so that people look at you as the expert and the authority. We've covered your content, so when an investor reviews it, they say, "This deal looks great. All the numbers line up. This is something that works for me. Let's go.'

Now that they've committed, you've got to get them to close. Your confidence is through the roof because your content is good, you've got major credibility, you're in the right state of mind. In the sequence I teach, you send out your investor packet to as many people as you possibly can. The reason why it is important to do this is that it causes SCARCITY and URGENCY. If you send out a deal and people know it is first-come, first served, what you're doing is you're saying there's not enough to go around for all of you. There's only one person who will be able to do this deal with me.

Create that scarcity. The potential investor has to hurry. When you send that Investor Packet off to one person and they commit, it is a great feeling when all these other people come running. You are happy when you have to say, "That deal has been taken. Be sure you act quickly next time." In fact that is the best feeling in the world, other than making love to your significant other, to have to say the sentence "That one is spoken for, be ready for the next one"

This is how you close a deal. The people who didn't get the deal will say, "Send it to me next time if it looks anything like this one. I am for sure in." Then, they'll tell their friends, and it spreads like wildfire when you do good by people. Even if they don't make a ton of money but you were honest with them, they'll want to do business with you because you've shown you're trustworthy and hardworking.

The Approach

The approach is important. There are two different approaches for people you are familiar with versus people you are unfamiliar with. If you're unfamiliar with a potential investor, they're going to say, "Hey, what do you do?" or "What are you up to?" or "What kind of things are you into?" That's where you provide two or three lines to pique their interest, something like, "I grow money."

Let's say you're on a plane, at a basketball game, or at your kid's game. You're sitting there with Baseball Dad and Soccer Mom, and they ask, "What do you do?" There are a couple of lines that I find that work well. You could say, "I grow money," and they say, "What? What do you mean 'you grow money?'" You reply, "People invest money with me and I grow it for them through real estate deals." Then, you leave it alone.

Or you could say, "I run an army of money. We have all these little soldiers out there making more soldiers and cloning themselves. We invest in real estate and it keeps growing." You want people to say, "Wait, what?" Don't just say, "I invest in real estate." That's boring. Don't be boring! The boring person gets passed over. Be the person who is passionate, excited, pumped about what you're doing. What you are doing here is you're dropping seeds. They may not come to fruition now but they will later. You may not have a deal now but you want to get their interest piqued.

So, you piqued their interest with something like, "I grow money in real estate, and we get our investors amazing returns." They say, "Wow, tell me more." That's when you've got them! You throw in, "I supervise or lead…"

I like the word *lead*. You're saying something that is going to catch their attention. "It's beautiful. Let me know if you're ever interested." You always have to say, whether the person you are talking with is unfamiliar or familiar, "Let me know if you're ever interested," and then you leave it alone.

If they're not interested, they will drop the subject. This is fine because you don't want to hard-sell them. If they are interested, they'll ask something like, "Is it difficult or risky?" Then you can elaborate: "No, I've created a safe system. It's pretty quick. My friends all do it; we've been doing it for 12 years." Or, if you're new, you can say, "My partners and I have been doing it for a while." They may ask, "Who are your partners?" Don't panic. I'm now the CIO of your company, the Chief Information Officer. I have a lot more information than you do and I'm pouring it into you. If you're working with me, you can email me your deal. I will look it over and say, "Yeah, that's good; go forth and conquer, my friend."

If the person you are talking to wants more details, you can say something like, "Well, we've been making double-digit returns on our real estate deals." Again, leave them with, "Let me know if you are interested." The reason for this is because you don't want to talk to them about it if they're not genuinely interested. This takes your anxiety level too high for no reason. In the beginning, you're super nervous about talking to people because you're afraid of the outcome. If your anxiety level is a nine out of ten it is because you're trying to close them right then and there. But if you're simply asking, "Yeah, if you're ever interested, let me know," it drops the anxiety index down to about a two or a three. Why? Because you're NOT trying to close them right there.

Educate

This is the mentality; this is how we close. We all want to be led down a path. Your potential investors are thinking, "What can I get here? Can I get from A to Z? Awesome. Show me how I can do it. If I can do this from A to Z, that's where I want to go. I can't make a decision right here; show me and educate me first."

A lot of people say, "I'm not good at sales." You don't have to be. Just educate. "Hey, this is what I'm doing. What do you do? Where is your money growing right now?" They'll say, "Ugh, it hasn't been growing a whole lot; I've been making one or two percent." "Oh, that's too bad. Some investors with me are making double-digit returns. Let me know if you're ever interested."

It's got to be cool. It has to be casual if you want to close. All the best closers, the people who are the best at raising private money do not say, "Please, I need you." They're like, "Hey this is what we're doing. If you're interested, let's go." I've raised a lot of private money. This is how I did it. It wasn't the quick close. Instead, you are slowly turning the unfamiliar person into someone familiar. Now, they may say, "I'm super interested!" You have to resist the urge to vomit on them everything you know about real estate. Why? I understand the temptation to let them know everything you've learned. But if you start to qualify yourself to them, you become weaker in position when it comes to negotiation. If you start with, "I'm this, I'm this, I'm this," they're going to be like, "Why is this person trying to qualify themselves so much to me? Why are you trying so hard to win me over? Maybe this isn't good."

We have a negative association in our mind about borrowing money. We just do. It's our culture; it's our society. It's the way we are. So, when someone says, "Hey can I borrow money?" we're like, "Why? What for? What do you mean? How are you going to pay me back?" Change the conversation to, "Hey, I've got an opportunity for you."

Good News

The reason we use the term *close* is that it sounds so "sales-y." Maybe you're thinking, "I don't know that I like that term." Let me tell you why we use it: ultimately, it's not a bad thing to close people. If it's a good investment, closing them is the best thing you can do for them. Now, they're making two percent on their investment. You can make them ten or twelve percent. Is that a good thing or a bad thing? It's a great thing! You have an outstanding opportunity; you're going to make them a lot more money. What's the negative thing here? It sounds too good to be true. It can't be too good to be true when people are making double digits in real estate every single day. The reason why people don't do it is that they don't know about it. When they don't know about it, they don't have the opportunity.

You arrive as the bearer of good news. If you're simply sharing the good news of the opportunity and letting them come, you're no longer super anxious. It is okay if you're nervous because you haven't done it a whole lot. But you say to them, "I've got an awesome opportunity. If you're interested, I'm happy to show you what we do. Let me know." When you hear, "Yes, I'm super interested," that's where you say, "When I get another deal coming across my desk, I'll send it your way. I will show you how we can make some money together."

Always remember this: "I will show you how we can make some money together." It's never about, "I need your money with my project so *I* can make money." Everybody has dialed into WIIFM: What's In It For Me. Remember, when you're talking with a potential private investor to focus on what's in it for them. How can you serve them?

The more your heart is to serve, to help, to be a blessing to others, the more you're going to be served, helped and blessed yourself. It is the way it is.

With that in mind, the key message of your close is, "Listen, I want to help you. I want to do things that will benefit us together. If it benefits you, it benefits me." If it doesn't benefit them at all and only benefits you, your relationship will be short-lived.

I know you're anxious because I was at one point, too. But when I realized I wasn't trying to convert them to my religion, so to speak, I was just planting a seed and letting them, see what I do, I relaxed. They'll take a while. They have their own negative hang-ups as well. You don't know where they're at; you don't know what their mindset is. They might think real estate is the worst thing that could ever happen to anybody in their entire life. Should you take that personally? No. It's not about you. You just presented them with an opportunity. If they're interested, cool; if they're not, it's no big deal. Next.

If a potential investor wants more information and asks, "What exactly do you do?" say, "I buy distressed homes, I fix them up, and flip them for the profit. I buy distressed assets, I fix them up, and I flip them for a profit." Say it over and over. The more confident and comfortable you are, the more it rolls off your tongue, and the more natural you sound. The more natural you sound the more comfortable people are going to be with you.

The People You Know

You might be thinking that you already know a lot of people with a lot of money. But a lot of times, the familiar people are some of the hardest for you to convert because they know you. Maybe they know you've had some failed business ventures in the past. But as you succeed more and more, you'll find that the familiar people will start coming out of the woodwork and say, "I'm interested in this. I've got some cash I'd like to put to work. You seem to be doing well; I'm game." That's great. You're going to see these people at family barbeques, family functions, Thanksgiving, Christmas. This causes a lot of anxiety for people because first of all, you don't want to lose their money. You don't want to have an awkward situation. You don't want to have that situation where you've lost somebody's money and then have to sit across from them at the Thanksgiving table.

So, here's how you approach it. When they ask you, "Hey, what have you been up to?" you say, "I'm working on real estate deals to make double-digit returns. If you're interested, let me know." Plant the seed. You don't have to answer every question. You don't want to get into a big brawl over why they should invest with you. It's only going to push them away. If you push, push, push, and press, people will run. You want to attract them. For example, if I have deals and I've let somebody know, "I got a bunch of other people looking at it. If you don't fund it, no big deal, but I wanted to give you the opportunity," they might come back and say, "If you're doing so well, why don't you fund it yourself?"

simply reply, "I will fund it myself but I wanted to give you the opportunity to make money with me. If you don't want to, no big deal."

I'm not going to get into a verbal argument to try and get somebody in. It never works that way. They have to come because they want to. Then I say, "I'll send you something over. Whenever I get another deal across my desk, I'll send you it over and we can see how we can make money together."

Also remember that even billionaires raise money. They use Other Peoples Money, AKA OPM, to do more deals than they could by themselves.

What happens if a week goes by and you don't send them anything? They contact you and say, "Hey, I thought you were going to send me something; I'm interested." That's great. Who is pursuing who now? They're pursuing you. Now you're in the driver's seat. Do your darnedest to make sure you drive that car as best you possibly can to make them some money.

I used to have this total negative feeling that if I hit somebody up and asked if they wanted to do a deal with me that I'd look like the person selling Pampered Chef or prepaid phone cards. I was telling myself I was like a network marketer trying to get all my family and friends in. I never wanted to be that person. I don't think you want to be that person either and so that's why I developed this system. Don't worry too much about your family and friends. Go to familiar environments of people that like investing in real estate:

- Seminars
- Conferences
- Clubs
- Craigslist
- Escrow and Title Agents
- Realtors/Brokers

Go to the people who are saying, "I want to lend, I want to lend." Build your momentum with these people, because momentum makes things easier. So, when familiar people come and say, "You've been doing so well, you seem so happy...what are you up to?" the conversation is easy and natural. Everybody wants to hear about, learn about, and know about real estate.

So, when you do get a deal, what happens next? You send over the Investor Packet and it presents the deal for you: "Hey, I'm sending this over, get back to me. If you're not interested, no problem. I've got some other people interested." It's called SCARCITY and it's so powerful. We don't want anything being taken away from us. We have a great opportunity and we don't want it taken away.

Deposit Fee

Most people don't know how to create their own opportunities, so when a good one comes along, they want
to jump on it. Ninety-nine percent of the world does
not know how to create their own opportunity, so if
you create it for them, they're ready to jump on it.
Send them over an Investor Packet. They see it and they
think, "I'm in. This is awesome." Perfect. Here's what's
going to happen next. Sometimes you need to wire the
EMD; sometimes we need to get the mortgage together. Sometimes, I'll charge a $5,000.00 fee that will go
toward the construction cost as a good-faith deposit. To
explain it, say, "Listen, I can't have you back out because
I've got these deals to close. So, I'm going to have you
send in $5,000.00. It's a non-refundable fee that will go
towards the construction of the particular house. If you
back out, you're backing away from $5,000.00 and I'm
not left in a lurch."

That's something that I've used because I've created a
position and a persona that says, "If you're serious about
investing with me, I don't have any time to sit and then
hope you're going to come through." When you do close
a deal, your message is, "I am super excited, this is going
to be awesome; we're going to have some fun with this,

we're going to flip this property and we'll make some cash and we're going to celebrate!"

Make it fun. Be upbeat. Be a leader. Then do your absolute darnedest to make sure that they make money. Do everything you possibly can.

Follow these steps. You're going to feel uncomfortable at first, but that is okay. Action-takers are money makers. I saw a quote the other day that I liked: "Good things don't come to those who wait. Good things come to those who hustle. Those who wait get the leftovers."

The close is simple. Drop your anxiety because you're planting seeds and letting investors come to you. You're NOT desperate; you're in no hurry. Go out there and raise tons and tons of cash for your deals and be sure you tell me all about it because I want to hear your stories. I want to know what you're doing.

Email me at keith@keithyackey.com with all your successes, I love hearing about them.

Action Step

- When you're uncomfortable, that's when you're growing. Ask a friend, a family member, anybody you want, "If someone presented you with an opportunity to make good money investing in real estate, would you be interested?" As you ask, you'll get more and more comfortable talking about the topic. It's almost like you're taking a poll. It shows you how simple it can be.

COLLABORATION

The Holy Grail of investing is collaboration. I Call it Private Money Nirvana. Let me define what I mean when I say collaboration. Collaboration is when private investors who have gotten great returns with you and enjoyed a positive experience start to recruit their friends who also want to do deals together. Early in my career, I had flipped about 50 houses. A relative of mine had a father who was quite wealthy.

One of his friends went to that man and said, "Hey, I'd like to do some investing." He said, "If I was going to invest in real estate, I would want to do it with Keith." So, his son said, "My dad's looking to invest in real estate. He sees all the great work that you're doing. He'd love to jump on board."

I had a conversation with him. Next thing you know, he sends down his guy who runs all of his investments. They formed this group of about six individuals, all who had quite a bit of cash. The group wrote a check for $1.5 million.

That is collaboration. It is what will put gas on your investment fire faster than anything else. So, treat your investors well. Give them the good news and the bad news. Work your ass off to make sure things happen the way you say they will. Because when you do, they'll go find others. Remember, the long game here is doing right by your investors so they will bring you more cash than you'll ever need.

Reaching Private Money Nirvana

Collaboration is the last frontier in your private money journey. Actually, when I look at collaboration, I see it as private money nirvana. This simply means that when you've treated your investors well, they will collaborate with you on future deals and bring other investors to you as well. In fact, when new clients work with me, if they've already been doing deals, the first thing I ask is, "Have you gone back to the investors that you've already give great returns?" Ask those investors if they have friends that would like to be getting the same types of returns. Most people like to brag about their successes, their wins. Often, they've already been telling some people about you.

You might have this collaboration effect happening for you right now. Nevertheless, I would highly encourage you to make it set a part of your process. After you get a private money investor a good return on a deal, made it your policy to then ask, "Do you know anybody else who would like to do deals with us? We've got a lot of deal flow and are always looking for more people like you." Ask the question. They can say no, they can think to themselves, "I'm going to keep this to myself. But it is more more likely they will respond, "Yes, I actually do know a couple of people."

At that point, have *them* introduce you. You don't want them to give you a phone number and say, "Here, call this guy," because now you're calling out of the blue. That approach never frames you as an expert. It doesn't position you that well. Make sure your investor introduces you to that friend. Have *them* tell their story to this friend ahead of time. This lays out the red carpet for you. Then, when you do actually meet, you can talk candidly and openly. The right introduction allows you to be a little bolder in your approach because now all the doubt about the results you can offer has all been eliminated.

To get to private money nirvana, the place where you have more than enough funding to make any deal happen, you need to ask for referrals from existing investors. You got them a big win and they were a joy to work with. So, ask the question, "Who do you know?" Let's say your first private money investor has $300,000. They probably know two or three other people with that amount who are interested in doing the same thing. That's how $300,000 becomes $900,000. You'll soon be thinking, "I've got too much money. I need to go find more deals."

If you've got too many deals, you need more money. If you've got too much money, you need more deals. That's the two tracks of this game that you'll always be navigating.

Action Step:

- Ask your current private money investor to introduce you to one or two friends who might be interested in funding future projects together.

BONUS STRATEGIES

The strategy I want to explain right now can be so powerful. It's the self-directed IRA. I'm not a self-directed IRA expert, but I know people who are actual custodians. They can help you take whatever retirement plan you are in and move it into what's called the self-directed IRA. Basically, it's your individual retirement account that you can direct into real estate investments.

Some of you might be sitting on hundreds of thousands of dollars you had no idea you had access to. You are sitting on a goldmine to jumpstart your career, to fund deals—not only your deals but other deals as well. With a self-directed IRA, you actually have checkbook control over that account. Rather than let some guy put your money in hedge funds or mutual funds or whatever, you actually can put it into a real estate deal.

When people use this strategy, it can launch their career faster than they ever thought possible. When I share this during live events, people say, "Oh my gosh! I am sitting on actual fuel to power my real estate investing career. Not only that but I'm sitting on so much of it, I'd rather put it into the deals of others." They can make a much better return on the money that's just sitting there making a percent or two in some mutual fund.

I want to make you aware of the self-directed IRA. I can refer you to an expert guide. Email support@keithyackey.com so we can recommend that individual to you. I want you to use all the tools in your toolbox.

Some of you are in non-profit organizations. Some of you are in different types of self-employment plans. There are many different individual retirement accounts. I want to make sure that you are getting the best advice on what you are doing so you can jumpstart your career much faster than you ever thought possible.

Look into self-directed IRAs. Get your funds transferred over so you can use that money to fund the deals that are going on all around you. Use it to go live the life of your dreams by raising all the private money you can possibly ever need and do the deals you want.

Be Aware of the Law

You have to be very careful when you are dealing with raising private money due to federal and state laws. The Securities and Exchange Commission, the SEC, created some rules during the Depression of the 1930s to protect investors who are not sophisticated. They have a lot of rules regarding prior relationships and whether you are openly soliciting people with unregistered securities. It's a big deal and you can violate a lot of these SEC regulations and get major trouble if you're not aware of the rules. I want you to try and steer clear of this. I'm not an SEC attorney, but I can put you in touch with one. You should work with an attorney. Lending laws are different in every one of these states and lending laws are different in states if you cross state lines.

There's a thing out there called Regulation D. It has exemptions for the dollar amount that you have and how many investors you can raise into a fund per those dollar amounts. I won't get into all the details of that law specifically, except to say you have to be careful in how you word things. For example, you can't just put up a billboard that says, "Invest with me and I am going to give you 12% guaranteed return."

Never say the word *guarantee* ever.

Create a relationship with people based on what you do. When you are posting on Craigslist, you can offer free education on what it's like to invest in mortgages or what it's like to invest in deeds of trust. By offering this free information, you can say, "Anybody who wants to learn how to invest in deeds of trust or mortgages, contact me. We'll have a chat." You can go literally sit down with them and show them, what it's like to invest in deeds of trust. That way they could become sophisticated or at least have some knowledge of what's happening. Meanwhile, you are building that relationship before you say, "Hey, let's invest in some deals together."

A lot of people are unaware of the SEC. I encourage you to talk to an attorney in your state who is familiar with dealing with the SEC guidelines. Some of you are going to be taking this game to a bigger level than others. Maybe you will put together a large fund or put a private place memorandum together. That's where you are going to have to talk to your attorney. That way you are not getting led astray or getting faulty information. In fact, talk to three attorneys. I did business with one, and he was expensive. I realized I could have gotten that same document for a quarter of the price. We are talking a six-figure price for a private place memorandum and getting a fund together to go buy big apartments. So, be aware of that.

Always check with your attorney. If you are putting together any fund or deal and you are nervous at all, reach out to an attorney who is an expert at the SEC. Talk to experts.

Your Attorney Could Turn into Your Investor

An investor friend of mine was thinking about how he could raise money. Where can he raise money? I said, "Why don't you get a deal together, send it to a real estate attorney in your city, and have that real estate attorney look over your deal? Put it under the auspices of, 'Will you look this deal over for me to make sure it's a good deal?'" Then once the attorney looks it over, go into his office and drop of the Investor Packet.

It's probably only going to take him 15 minutes to look it over so it may only cost you $150. Here's what happens. When he is looking it over and he says, "This is an amazing deal, you should do it," look him straight in the eyes and say, "Cool. I want you to fund it." This actually happened to one of my clients. The attorney replied, "Absolutely. I will make more money funding this deal for you than I would just looking it over."

My client landed that attorney. They did that deal because a real estate attorney knows what he is looking at. He looks at it and says, "You are buying this distressed asset for this price and you are going to fix it up for this amount, and you are going to sell it for this price, and I'm going to put the money up. We are going to split this profit 50-50."

The reason I told my client to go to a real estate attorney is that's what these professionals deal with day in and day out. They understand mortgages, deeds, all of it. It doesn't hit an attorney by surprise. I always start with the real estate attorney. But what happened in this situation was this guy landed that attorney. Lawyers have been flipping property forever. It's the hobby of the rich. The attorney in my story made a great return and who do you think he told? He told his attorney buddy. This turned into a little attorney ring of private funding for my student.

Think outside the box. You never know what could happen. Nothing ventured, nothing gained guys. When my clients go to 15, 20, or 30 attorneys, they always find at least one attorney who is highly interested. If the deal is right, they say, "I like this deal and if you have anything more like this, send them my way."

First Meeting

A little tip I want to share for when it's time for you to meet an investor in person. That first meeting can be a little nerve-wracking especially for those of you who are just starting. You will always remember the first meeting, but you have to go through the first meeting before you can get to the fifth. Here is what you do: find out are you are truly a good fit for each other. Ask them questions.

I'll tell you a story about how I majorly botched a big opportunity with somebody who had a lot of money. I didn't find out what they were looking for, what they needed, or what they were expecting. Therefore, we were in two totally different worlds. We never did any business together. I didn't get the right information out of him. So, be sure to ask, "Where's your money right now? What is it making right now?"

If I find out you are earning 15% a year, I may not be able to compete with that. Find out. If they say, "I'm investing in mutual funds," just say, "Awesome. What kind of yearly return are you getting on that money?" "Well, I'm getting a 4% return."

You are taking their temperature. If you just go right in and say, "I'll give you 10% return on the deal," and they are used to getting 15%, then they are going to say no. But if you go in and try offering a 10% return and they are used to getting 4%, you probably could have done business at 6 or 7%. You are leaving money on the table.

Unless you start asking questions, you'll lose out. Say, "Hey! What are you doing? What kind of money are you making on your money right now? Are you happy with it? Are you satisfied with what's happening right now?" You are getting them to divulge the information about what they are excited about. If you start asking questions, you might feel uncomfortable. These questions can be a little bit odd at first because you are not used to asking these types of questions to people. But if you position yourself as the expert who will give them an opportunity, then you have to know the answers to these questions: "Hey, where's your money invested right now? What kind of return are you making on it right now?"

The next question you should be asking is, "What are your expectations of our relationship? What are your expectations of return you can make with me?" If you posted an ad that showed a deal and they saw the actual expectations of that deal, then they are probably going to regurgitate your ad copy to you. They might reply, "I saw your ad that you are giving a 12% return or 15% return." When you receive this answer, you have an understanding of what's going on. You understand what you can offer them.

Once you get to know the investor and understand their expectation, say, "Let me take this information and think about a deal. I will see if this is something that will be a good fit for you and me." I've found that when you say, "Let me see if this is a good fit for you and me," what you are basically saying is, "I'm not sure if this is a good fit. I'm qualifying you more than you are necessarily qualifying me," that flips the script. Most people aren't used to hearing that.

Most people who are bad at raising private money are saying, "Oh my gosh, I need money. I've got this deal and if you don't fund it then I'm going to go broke and I'm going to die and the whole worlds going to fall apart." It's much better to simply say, "Hey! This might be a fit. I'm not sure if it is or not. I'm just asking questions." That takes your anxiety index down as you are just asking questions. Because if it is a fit, then you both are going to want to do lots of business together.

That first meeting? Ask questions. Explore. Find out what they are expecting. Maybe there is the possibility of a fit, maybe there's not. Not everybody who wants to raise private money or everybody who has private money to invest in your real estate deal is a match, for whatever reason. Who knows? Maybe their father went bankrupt doing real estate deals. Don't take a "no" personally.

I highly encourage you to get as many meetings as you possibly can because the more meetings you get, the more people you will find who click with you and want to fund your deals.

Action Step

- Ask questions. Find out what the investor's expectations might include. Be cordial, be friendly,
  and then leave it at that.

RAISING MONEY

I was flipping single-family residences and it was going fantastically well. In addition to flipping, I owned about 80 single-family residences and was bringing in cash flow via rental payment. I was loving it, so I got involved in the apartment game. The very first fourplex I ever bought was a property I acquired at an auction to buy single-family residences. I was there with my business partner and this fourplex came up. I thought to myself, "I want to own a fourplex." Its price seemed too low. I thought, "How can I pass up on such a good deal?" It was down to me and a lady. It was just us at the final bid and the price was around $67,000. Going once, going twice. That was her bid. My partner said, "Let it go. It's too much." Instead of listening to him, I said, "68!"

I got it for $68k. I was so pumped that I got that fourplex. I was going to give a $5,000 deposit on top of it for buying at the auction. So, I went outside to call my realtor. I said, "Listen, I just got this property. It's a fourplex with some fire damage. It's going to need some pretty extensive renovation but please tell me what you think it's worth." He said, "Well, it's been on the market for a while. I'd say maybe $55,000," My heart sunk. I said, "Wait, you are telling me I could have bought it for $55,000 and I just bought it at the auction for $68,000 plus $5,000?" I had just paid $73,000. I realized my partner was never going to let me live it down.

I called my banker the next day and said, "Hey! I got this fourplex and I'm going to renovate it. What do you think it's going to be worth when it's all renovated?" He did his calculations, looked at a desktop appraisal, and said, "We think it's worth about $200,000 because of the value of the rent. We'll give you a loan for $130,000."

Excuse me?

"Yes, we'll give you a loan that amount. Here are the terms." I called my partner and said, "You are not going to believe this. We are in the thing for $73,000 and it will cost about $30-35k to fix up. They are going to give us a loan for $130k, and once the thing is rented, it will cover the debt service and cash flow for about $900 a month. We get to own this property, renovate this property, stick a big chunk of cash in our pocket and the thing is going cash flow every single month."

I was pretty excited. I literally bought 13 more properties like that one during the next three months. Why? Because they were such good deals. As I started accumulating these fourplexes, it dawned on me: what if I just bought a bunch of these complexes together? I bought an eightplex, then a couple of ten-plexes, then a twelveplex. You get the idea. It just kept building.

I got more and more comfortable with it. Maybe you are interested in the apartment game. I think raising money for these types of things is a lot of fun because owning a lot of doors results in a lot of cash flow coming in. I want to show you how I structured these deals and exactly what I did so you could structure your deals the same way. Rather than just doing a single property through your cooperation or your LLC and having the investor fund the escrow, these types of deals are a little bit different.

Apartment Investing

First, consult with your SEC attorney. I know I talked a little bit about this in the last chapter, but this is something you must do. Accredited investors are savvy investors and that's who you'll be dealing with here. You can't just go out there and say, "I'm putting a fund together for apartments." The way you are going to raise money for apartments is different than the way you raise money for single-family residences. The way I did it almost 100% of the time was to form an LLC. Then, investors would fund the LLC, like we were starting a business together. The LLC is the legal entity that buys the properties, whether it is one fourplex, an eightplex, or whatever. You can do this for single-family residences as well.

When you actually form an LLC, private money investors are going to do a capital contribution to start that business. Next, you must fill out an operating agreement. An operating agreement is simply how the LLC is going to operate.

You are going to be a 1% owner; they are going to be a 99% owner. The reason for that is simply this: If they do capital contribution to your LLC and you are 50-50 partners, it's as if you own 50% of the equity that has been invested into the LLC. You now own half of what they contributed, which you don't. You own half of the upside or you own a portion of the profits that the cash spins off from those rents. You don't own half of the LLC, so you have to write it out. One percent manager, 99% non-manager. You are going to be the 1%.

Next, break down in the operating agreement where the rents go first when they come in each month. Note where they go second, where they go third. Write down what the preferred return is. When you are dealing with apartments and investors, you are offering those investors a preferred return. Preferred return simply means that you are giving them a return first. Any of the cash flow that comes in will first go to taxes and insurance. Then, the next portion will go to your property management company. Then whatever is left over is distributed according to that preferred return agreement. For example, let's say the investor puts in $100,000. It's a small number but it's good for this example. You've agreed to give them a six percent preferred return. That means after the LLC has paid the taxes, insurance, and property management, the first $6,000 goes to the investor. That amount is six percent of $100,000.

Usually, we disperse on a quarterly basis. Every three months, they get a quarterly check for $1,500. If there's any cash over that, you can put in the operating agreement that you and that investor split that cashflow 50-50. Let's say that when everything is all said and done, there's $8,000 at the end of the year. Because $6,000 is the preferred return, that amount goes to them. Then there's another $2,000 left. $1,000 goes to them, $1,000 goes to you. That's called splitting the profits.

Write in the operating agreement that when you go to sell the property, whatever cash they had invested in that deal to buy the property, renovate the property, and get the property rented, they will get back. They get all of their initial investment—called their basis—back.

Then, if you agree to split the sales profit 50-50, that means 50% will go to them, 50% will go to you.

You own 1%, they own 99% even though you are going to get 50% of the profits when you go to sell the property. That is, legally, how you want to write this out. Obviously, you are going to have to pay the taxes, the insurance, and the property management fees first. You will have to pay legal fees. Then, when you go to sell that property, it's called disposition of the property, they get their initial investment back. You then split the profit 50-50.

Asset Management

I want to explain something called an asset management fee. When you put this entire fund together, you are the asset manager. You've probably heard the term "asset manager" a lot. Well, now that's going to be you. You will charge 1% or 2% for performing this job. Both are perfectly normal fees for putting an entire fund together. You get 1% right off the top. Sometimes you can make that an annual 1%.

Remember, you are not the property manager. You do not want to be the property manager. You are the asset manager, meaning you are making sure that the asset is doing what it's supposed to do. You are going to make sure that the houses are getting purchased when they are supposed to. They are getting renovated the way they are supposed to. They are getting rented. You are keeping track of the property manager, making sure everything is getting leased the way it's supposed to be. Then, you are making sure that the taxes are being paid. You are making sure that the asset is running the way it is supposed to be run. You are making sure that the accounting is good.

When you are building your investor packet, you are doing the same things. Remember the only two things in apartments that can make you more money: 1) increasing the income, or 2) decreasing the expenses. It is just like any other business. As the asset manager, it is your job to show how you can increase the rent and decrease the expense so there's more profitability. It's your job to decide if you can generate extra income by adding a laundry area, paid parking, or vending machines.

This isn't a book on how to invest in apartments but these are the things you have to be thinking through as you are raising money for these deals. Show a projection of how much rent is coming in, what the possible appreciation of these properties is, what their cash-on-cash return is going to be, etc. Then, if you sell for a bigger profit down the road, and you divide it by the years that you held the property, what is the ROI? And ultimately what is the Internal rate of return for the whole life of the asset.

With an apartment fund, you are simply addressing accredited investors who want to put money into an LLC. Write that LLC with the operating agreement. I want you to talk with your SEC attorney, your real estate attorney, and make sure that your LLC and your operating agreement is exactly how it's supposed to be for your state. Always be compliant with the law. If you have a question, ask your SEC attorney.

Action Steps

- Have a real estate attorney look over your operating agreement for the apartment fund LLC.
- Sit down in front of some investors and show them a long-term hold investment packet.
- If you have questions, send a message to support@keithyackey.com. I can't wait to see you at the live event.

Finally in closing, you will do best by hiring a coach to help you do this. I have hired a coach in everything I have ever done. It is no secret that I am successful. The reason for that is simple, I have great coaching. And you can too! To find out more about raising private money and having me coach you to becoming a pro at this go to www.PrivateMoneySecretsBook.com/Message

and watch a very important video I have made for you there.

Your dreams are important and worth fighting for. Don't ever give up and don't ever listen to anyone who tells you that you cannot do this. You CAN! I did and so can YOU!

Keith

Ready to Explode Your
Real Estate Investing Business?

Get IMMEDIATE Access to a

FREE

"Private Money Secrets"
On-Demand Class Today!

www.PrivateMoneySecretsBook.com/class

www.ingramcontent.com/pod-product-compliance
Lightning Source LLC
Chambersburg PA
CBHW061156240326
R18026500001B/R180265PG41519CBX00007B/7